SCRIBES AND TRANSLATORS

SUPPLEMENTS

TO

VETUS TESTAMENTUM

EDITED BY
THE BOARD OF THE QUARTERLY

VOLUME LIV

SCRIBES AND TRANSLATORS

SEPTUAGINT AND OLD LATIN IN THE BOOKS OF KINGS

BY

NATALIO FERNÁNDEZ MARCOS

E.J. BRILL

LEIDEN · NEW YORK · KÖLN

1994

The paper in this book meets the guidelines for permanence and durability of the Committee on Production Guidelines for Book Longevity of the Council on Library Resources.

Library of Congress Cataloging-in-Publication Data

Fernández Marcos, N.
    Scribes and translators : Septuagint and Old Latin in the Books of Kings / by Natalio Fernández Marcos.
      p.   cm. — (Supplements to Vetus Testamentum, ISSN 0083-5889 ; v. 54)
    "The Grinfield Lectures 1991 and 1992 ... at the University of Oxford"—Pref.
    Includes bibliographical references and indexes.
    ISBN 9004100431 (alk. paper)
    1. Bible. O.T. Kings—Versions.   I. Title. II. Title: Grinfield lectures. III. Series.
BS410.V452 vol. 54
[BS1335.2]
222'.5048—dc20
                                        94-9717
                                         CIP

Die Deutsche Bibliothek - CIP-Einheitsaufnahme

Fernández Marcos, Natalio:
Scribes and translators : Septuagint and old Latin in the Books of kings / by Natalio Fernández Marcos. - Leiden ; New York ; Köln : Brill, 1994
    (Supplements to Vetus testamentum ; Vol. 54)
    ISBN 90-04-10043-1
NE: Vetus testamentum / Supplements

ISSN 0083-5889
ISBN 90 04 10043 1

PRINTED IN THE NETHERLANDS

CONTENTS

PREFACE

The present volume reproduces, with slight modifications, the Grinfield Lectures 1991 and 1992 which I had the honour to deliver at the University of Oxford.

My thanks go to the University of Oxford for their invitation to give this Lecturership on the Septuagint version of the Hebrew Bible. In particular I want thank Professor Sebastian Brock for his warm hospitality and all those who attended the Lectures at the Oriental Institute for their helpful comments, especially M.P. Goodman, H.G.M. Williamson, C. Mango, P. Wernberg-Møller, A. Salvesen and D. Taylor.

I remember with gratitude all the members of Campion Hall, who made me feel at home during my stay in Oxford. I am especially grateful to the Master, Joseph A. Munitiz, to whom I am indebted for the stylistic revision of these Lectures.

Last but not least, I would like to thank E.J. Brill Publishers of Leiden as well as the Editorial Board of the Supplements to *Vetus Testamentum* for accepting this volume for publication.

At a time when so much emphasis is placed on the publication of the Qumran Documents, it is perhaps not inappropriate to remind the reader of the existence of other, some of them still unedited, witnesses that can also shed light on the textual history of the Bible.

N.F.M.

SIGLA AND ABBREVIATIONS

BASOR	Bulletin of the American Schools of Oriental Research.
Bib	Biblica, Roma.
BIOSCS	Bullettin of the International Organization for Septuagint and Cognate Studies.
CBQ	Catholic Biblical Quarterly, Washington, DC.
CCSL	Corpus Christianorum Series Latina, Turnhout.
EB	Estudios Bíblicos, Madrid.
GCS	Die Griechischen Christlichen Schriftsteller der ersten Jahrhunderte, Berlin.
Henoch	Henoch, Torino.
HSM	Harvard Semitic Monographs, Cambridge Mass.
IDBS	The Interpreter's Dictionary of the Bible. Supplementary Volume, Nashville.
JSOT	Journal for the Study of the Old Testament, Sheffield.
LXX	The Septuagint Version.
LXX rell.	The majority Text of the Septuagint as opposed to the Antiochene.
MT	The Masoretic Text.
nF	Neue Folge.
NTTS	New Testament Tools and Studies, Leiden.
OS	Oudtestamentische Studiën, Leiden.
OT	Old Testament.
PG	Migne, Patrologia Graeca.
PL	Migne, Patrologia Latina.
RB	Revue Biblique, Jerusalem.
RevBén	Revue Bénédictine, Maredsous.
RQ	Revue de Qumran, Paris.
SC	Sources Chrétiennes, Paris.
Sefarad	Sefarad, Madrid.
ST	Studi e Testi, Roma.
Textus	Textus, Jerusalem.
TLZ	Theologische Literaturzeitung, Berlin.
TR	Theologische Rundschau, Tübingen.
TU	Texte und Untersuchungen zur Geschichte der altchristlichen Literatur, Berlin.

VC   Vigiliae Christianae, Leiden.
VL   Vetus Latina.
VTS   Vetus Testamentum. Supplement, Leiden.
ZAW   Zeitschrift für die Alttestamentliche Wissenschaft, Berlin.
ZDMG   Zeitschrift der Deutschen Morgenländischen Gesellschaft, Wiesbaden.

THE SEPTUAGINT AND THE HISTORY OF
THE BIBLICAL TEXT

CHAPTER ONE

PAST AND PRESENT IN BIBLICAL TEXT HISTORY

For a Spanish student of the sixties Oxford was a dream, a dream that evoked almost an ideal climate of real scholarship and freedom in contrast with the crude reality of Spain, social as well as academic, of those years.

For a scholar and researcher of the Consejo Superior de Investigaciones Científicas (CSIC) of the early nineties, Oxford is still a dream, a mark of quality and excellency that calls for commitment from everyone who has the honour of lecturing in this venerable *Alma Mater*. Therefore I express my sincere thanks to the university and in particular to the persons responsible for the Grinfield Lectureship for my, in no way deserved, appointment.

It is a pleasure to remember on this occasion the ancient ties of friendship between my former teachers Prof. Pérez Castro and the late Díez Macho and a brilliant Professor of this university, Paul Kahle during the fifties. Among the other numerous honorary distinctions granted to this Professor, he was appointed in 1951 "Consejero de Honor del CSIC." Not only he, but the late Prof. Kilpatrick was in close contact too with the Department of Biblical studies in the CSIC of Madrid throughout the Program of the Biblia Políglota Matritense. And personally I acknowledge with gratitude my debt to Prof. Sebastian Brock and his Oxford Dissertation *The Recensions of the Septuagint Version of 1 Samuel* (1966), a study that, in spite of being on deposit in the Bodleian Library, has been much more quoted than most of the published monographs on this subject.

As editor of a text of the Septuagint, *The Antiochian Text of I-II Samuel*, I would like to propose some reflections on the text history of the Septuagint in the light of the new insights in the realm of textual criticism during the last decades since the Qumran Discoveries.

When Origen started work on his tremendous monument of Biblical text criticism, the Hexapla, his principal aim, was in all probability to provide Christians with an useful instrument for their controversy with the Jews[1]. However, from the bulk of his Biblical

---

[1] Cf. S.P. Brock, "Origen's aims as a Textual critic of the Old Testament". *Studia Patristica* X ed. F.L. Cross (= *TU* 107) Berlin 1970, 215-218 p. 216.

commentaries some remarks on the history of the Biblical text can be gleaned. Guided by the philological work of the Alexandrian grammarians, he wanted to compare the different copies of the Septuagint in order to attain the most exact equivalent of the Hebrew text[2]. As he was dealing with a translated text he did not dare to add or to omit anything because this procedure was at the root of the corruption caused by the copyists[3]. Instead of that he provided the text with asterisks and obelus, to indicate the minus and plus of the Septuagint in relation to the Hebrew. As a matter of fact the Hebrew text was the ultimate criterion of the genuine Septuagint. Of course most of the disagreements of the Septuagint with the Hebrew might be due to a careless text transmission of the different copies[4], but some of them might be the product of the translators in order to render more accurately the meaning of the passage in question[5], or might be due to a mystic reason that only God knows[6]. Moreover, Origen admits as quite possible another hypothesis: that the Hebrew copies might have been different from the contemporary ones[7].

---

[2] Cf. P. Nautin, *Origène. Sa vie et son oeuvre*, Paris 1977, p. 351-353.

[3] Origen, *Comm. in Matth. XV,14 (GCS 40,387)*: πολλὴ γέγονεν ἡ τῶν ἀντι-γράφων διαφορά. εἴτε ἀπὸ ῥαθυμίας τινῶν τῶν γραφέων, εἴτε ἀπὸ τόλμης τινῶν μοχθηρᾶς... εἴτε καὶ ἀπὸ τῶν τὰ ἑαυτοῖς δοκοῦντα ἐν τῇ διορθώσει <ἢ> προστιθέν-των ἢ ἀφαιρούντων (There was a great disagreement among the manuscripts, be it by carelessness of some copyists or evil audacity of others...be it because others added or omitted in the correction what they thought convenient).

[4] Origen, *Comm. in Matth. XV, 14.*

[5] Origen, *Comm. in Ps. 2,12 (PG 12,1116D)*: Ἀλλ' ἐπεὶ οὔτε ἐν τῷ Ἑβραικῷ πρόσκειται, οὔτε ἐν ταῖς λοιπαῖς ἑρμηνείαις τὸ δικαίας, ὑποπτεύομεν μήποτε ἢ κατ' οἰκονομίαν προσέθηκαν τοῦτο, ἢ τὰ ἀντίγραφα ἁμάρτηται (But because δικαίας lacks in the Hebrew and in the rest of the translations we suspect either that this has been added by divine dispensation or it is a mistake of the manuscripts).

[6] Origen, *Hom. in Hierem. 16,5,17.* Cf. P. Nautin, *Origène*, p. 352 and M. Harl, "Origène et la sémantique du langage biblique". *VC* 26,3 (1972) 161-188, p. 179-181; ——, "Origène et les interprétations patristiques grecques de l'obscurité biblique". *VC* 36,4 (1982) 334-372, p. 355.

[7] Origen, *Comm. in Ps. 3,8 (PG 12, 1129B)*: Τῷ Ἑβραικῷ ἐντυχόντες, τὸ ματαίως οὐδαμῶς εὕρομεν δυνάμενον δηλοῦσθαι. Τί γὰρ κοινὸν τῆς λέξεως τῆς ματαίως πρὸς τὴν σιαγόνα; Καὶ οἱ λοιποὶ δὲ ὡς τὸ Ἑβραικὸν τεθείκασιν. Εἰκὸς οὖν, ὥς τινες Ἑβραίων λέγουσι, τὰ ἀρχαῖα ἀντίγραφα ἑτέρως ἐσχηκέναι, ἢ τὸ εὐτελὲς περισταμέ-νους τοὺς Ἑβδομήκοντα τῆς λέξεως τετολμηκέναι ἀντὶ τοῦ σιαγόνα, ποιῆσαι ματαίως (Consulting the Hebrew it was impossible for us to explain ματαίως. For what has in common the word "in vain" with the "cheeck"?. The other translators put the same as the Hebrew. Probably the ancient manuscripts had a different reading, as some Jews say, or the Seventy avoiding a worthless statement dared to put "in vain" instead of "cheeck"). And in *Selecta in Ez. 7,27 (PG 13, 796)*: Τὸ Ὁ βασιλεὺς πενθήσει, συνηθῶς ἱστόρηται, τάχα διὰ τὸν Σωτῆρα οὐκ ἂν νομισθέντα πενθεῖν, οὐχ ἑρμηνευσάντων τῶν Ἑβδομήκοντα τὸ ῥητὸν, ἢ μὴ εὑρηκότων τότε ἐν τῷ Ἑβραικῷ τὴν

Occasionally the Septuagint might preserve the genuine reading while the corruption was to be attributed to the Hebrew copyists that became the source for the other editions. But the horizon of Origen's work was mainly apologetic, or at the utmost, that of the Alexandrian grammarians: a comparison of all the extant editions for the purpose of providing the Christians with the tools for their discussion with the Jews. As a byproduct one can gain some insights into the text history of the Bible.

Jerome's work as translator of the Bible is a practical consequence of the Hexapla, inasmuch as Origen's textual activity brought forth clearly the contamination of the whole Septuagint tradition[8]. Jerome's aim as translator of the Vulgata was to produce a translation more faithful to the *Hebraica veritas*, taking into account the textual dispersion of the *Trifaria varietas* and the corruption of the Septuagint tradition. In other words, Origen as well as Jerome, both outstanding representatives of the philological current in Christian antiquity, worked as textual critics with two presuppositions in mind: a) The original unity of the Biblical text and b) The priority of the Hebrew as the original language of the Bible.

In defense of his new translation Jerome describes, as Origen did a century before in defense of his critical work in the Hexapla, the miserable state of the biblical text now reflected in the extreme diversity of the Old Latin versions. Let us hear his own words in the Preface to the Book of Joshua: "*Maxime cum apud Latinos tot sint exemplaria quot codices, et unusquisque pro arbitrio suo vel addiderit vel subtraxerit quod ei visum est, et utique non possit verum esse quod dissonet*"[9]. Jerome attributes the differences among the manu-

---

λέξιν (The text ὁ βασιλεὺς πενθήσει is understood according to the common usage, perhaps because it is thought that the Saviour does not mourn, because the Seventy did not interpret such words or they did not find then such statement in the Hebrew).

[8] Cf. P. Wendland, "Zur ältesten Geschichte der Bibel in der Kirche". *ZAW* 1 (1900) 267-290, p. 284.

[9] Cf. Preface to Joshua in *Biblia Sacra iuxta Vulgatam Versionem* ed. R. Weber, I, Stuttgart 1975. second ed. p. 284. It is interesting to contrast this view of the textual criticism face to the background of other ideological presuppositions, for instance, unity of doctrine face to heresy. Jerome's last sentence, "et non possit verum esse quod dissonet" remind us another author, Epiphanius, well known for his catalogue of heresies. For him the differences of the biblical text from the variant readings cannot disturb the divine harmony. For Epiphanius even the asterised passages were in the original as present as the stars in the sky, although they may be obscured by the clouds. The basic insight of Tatian's *Diatessaron* was "that the truth

scripts to the activity of the copyists. The last sentence concerning the harmony of the Biblical text is the expression of a secular problem that arose the very day on which the first translation of the Bible was completed.

Jerome argues in favour of his new translation by also criticising the text transmission of the Septuagint. If we had the pure Septuagint just as it was translated, a new translation would be superfluous. But we find a Septuagint corrupted in many ways and diverse according to the different regions[10]. Therefore, in Jerome's opinion the disagreements among the Septuagint manuscripts arose from the accidents of the text transmission as well as from the existence of three major recensions of the Old Testament in Greek.

The disagreements of the Septuagint with the Hebrew are interpreted by Jerome too as accidents of textual transmission. The Hebrew original is therefore the ultimate criterion for any critical restoration and for his new translation. This becomes apparent in the *Preface to the book of Jeremiah* and in the *Preface to the book of Kings*[11].

He realises that the Septuagint of Ezechiel, in contrast with that of Jeremiah, does not disagree too much with the Hebrew and he wonders why the Greek translators being the same have translated at one time the same and, at another time different things[12]. Anyway he make the translators and later copyists responsible for the present disagreements with the Hebrew and for the corrupt passages. Jerome trusts the Hebrew and seems to have assumed that the current Hebrew text was identical with the *Vorlage* of the Septuagint. No doubt he was seduced by the impression of stability and uniformity of the Hebrew text of his time as compared with the variety of the Septuagint manuscripts and of the Old Latin versions[13]. In the

becomes visible only in unity and harmony'', cf. *Gospel Tradition in the Second Century*, ed. William L. Petersen, Notre Dame 1989.

[10] Preface to the Book of Chronicles. *Biblia Sacra iuxta Vulgatam Versionem* I,546.

[11] Preface to them Book of Jeremiah. *Biblia Sacra iuxta Vulgatam Versionem* II, p. 1166: "Praeterea ordinem visionum qui apud Graecos et Latinos omnino confusus est, ad pristinam fidem correximus", and Preface to the Books of Kings. *Biblia Sacra iuxta Vulgatam Versionem* I, p. 365-366: "Certe, si incredulus es, lege graecos codices et latinos et confer cum his opusculis, et ubicumque inter se videris discrepare, interroga quemlibet Hebraeorum cui magis accomodare debeas fidem".

[12] Preface to the Book of Ezechiel. *Biblia Sacra iuxta Vulgatam Versionem* II, p. 1266: "Sed et vulgata eius editio non multum distat ab hebraico. Unde satis miror quid causae extiterit, ut si eosdem in universis libris habemus interpretes, in aliis eadem, in aliis diversa transtulerint".

[13] Cf. B. Kedar, "The Latin Translations". In *Mikra. Text, Translations, Read-*

Renaissance it was the Septuagint that was mainly appreciated as the Bible of the Church Fathers and used as an instrument for recovering the right reading of the Vulgata, but there is no hint of its being used then as a path for recovering the original Hebrew[14].

As a matter of fact the critical value of the Septuagint for the restoration of the Hebrew was grasped by some scholars of the 19th century, as can be appreciated if one remembers in passing the names of Thenius, Wellhausen and Driver for the books of Samuel[15]. But ever since the Qumran discoveries we have witnessed for the first time important changes in the evaluation of the Greek Bible for the history of the Biblical text. It is not the moment to analyze minutely the impact of these writings—some of them still unpublished or not fully published—for the rethinking of the history of the Biblical text. A first mass of evidence consists of the new Greek documents coming from the Judaean Desert (7Q1LXX and 7Q2LXX; 4QLXXLev[a] and 4QLXXLev[b], 4QLXXNum, 4QLXXDeut) and especially the fragments of Dodekapropheton published by Barthélemy and recently reedited in the series of the Discoveries of the Judaean Desert by Tov-Kraft-Parsons[16]. These new witnesses have

---

ing and Interpretation of the Hebrew Bible in Ancient Judaism and Early Christianity, ed. M.J. Mulder, Van Gorcum 1988, 299-338, p.322: "It is interesting to note that Jerome, who permanently censured the Greek and Latin Bible texts, had utmost confidence in the reliability and constancy of the Hebrew; he seems to have assumed that the current Hebrew text-form was identical with that underlying the LXX. This can best be explained as consequence of the impression the relatively stabile text of the Hebrew OT made on any person who compared this situation with that prevailing in the area of the Greek and Latin versions".

[14] "Cardinal Carafa and his assistants rightly insisted on the value of the Septuagint for the right understanding of the use of Scripture by the Fathers and for the text of the Vulgate; but they do not appear to have grasped the value of the Septuagint for getting behind the Massoretic revision of the Hebrew text", cf. B. Hall, "Biblical Scholarship: editions and commentaries". In The Cambridge History of the Bible. The West From the Reformation to the Present Day, ed. S.L. Greenslade, Cambridge 1963, 38-94, p. 58.

[15] Cf. N. Fernández Marcos, "The Use of the Septuagint in the Criticism of the Hebrew Bible". Sefarad 47,1 (1987) 59-72, p. 60-61.

[16] 7Q1, pap 7QLXXExod (Rahlfs 805); 7Q2, pap 7QLXXEpJer (Rahlfs 804); 4Q119, 4QLXXLev[a] (Rahlfs 801); 4Q120, pap 4QLXXLev[b] (Rahlfs 802); 4Q121, 4QLXXNum (Rahlfs 803) and 4Q122, 4QLXXDeut (Rahlfs 819). Other pre-Christian witnesses of the Septuagint are Pap. Fouad 266 (Rahlfs 847 and 848) and Pap. Rylands 458 (Rahlfs 957). All of them are dated between the IInd century B.C. and the I[st] century A.D. Cf. D. Barthélemy, Les Devanciers d'Aquila. VTS X (1963); N. Fernández Marcos, "La Septuaginta y los hallazgos del Desierto de Judá". En Simposio Bíblico Nacional, Madrid 1984, p. 229-244; E. Ulrich, "The Greek Manuscripts of the Pentateuch from Qumrân, Including Newly-Identified

supported basically Lagarde's view of the origins of the Septuagint, as has been recognised by almost every Septuagint scholar, depriving Kahle's Targumic hypothesis of any actual evidence[17]. These documents exhibit a Septuagint agreeing (in a high proportion of cases) with the text of the main uncials four or fifth centuries before the copying of those manuscripts. In some cases these new witnesses from the Judaean Desert are so close in date to the translation that the co-existence of different translations can hardly be spoken of, a fact that has been rightly emphasized by many scholars[18]. While this basic original unity has been confirmed, at the same time some traces of textual revision, with the purpose to bring the Greek text into agreement with the Hebrew current in Palestine in the first century A.D. or to improve stylistically the Greek, can be discerned. In other words, the unity of the translation of the Pentateuch and *Dodekapropheton* seems to be confirmed, but there are sufficient signs that the revisional activity started almost as soon as the translation was completed, at least while the Septuagint was being transmitted within the Jewish community, and especially when nationalistic feeling renewed the use of the Hebrew language[19].

But for the text history of the Septuagint we cannot rely only on the Greek material recovered in the Judaean Desert. The new Hebrew texts of Qumran have influenced this area of research with

---

Fragments of Deuteronomy (4QLXXDeut)''. In *De Septuaginta. Studies in honour of John William Wevers on his sixty-fifth birthday*, ed. A. Pietersma and C. Cox, Toronto/ Brandon 1984, p. 71-85 and *The Greek Minor Prophets Scroll From Naḥal Ḥever (8ḤevXIIgr) (The Seiyâl Collection I)*, by Emanuel Tov with the collaboration of R.A. Kraft and a contribution by P.J. Parsons, Oxford 1990.

[17] It can be said that nowadays this is the general opinion of the Septuagint scholars in spite of Kahle's protest and interpretation of the Discoveries of the Judean Desert in favour of his theory, cf. P. Kahle, "Die im August 1952 entdeckte Lederrolle mit dem griechischen text der kleinen Propheten und das Problem der Septuaginta''. *TLZ* 79 (1954) 81-84 and ——, *The Cairo Geniza*, Oxford 1959, p. 226-228.

[18] Cf. John W. Wevers in *ThR* n.f. 33 (1968) p. 67: "Unser text (i.e. Dodekapropheton) sollte nun ein und für allemal Kahles Theorie von den 'vielen Übersetzungen' begraben''; and recently John W. Wevers, "Barthélemy and Proto-Septuagint Studies''. *BIOSCS* 21 (1988) 23-35, p. 31: "...it does reflect an overall picture of a text which has been extensively revised but at least two thirds of which has been left untouched and thus easily identified''. See for the Pentateuch E. Ulrich, "The Greek Manuscripts'' p. 82.

[19] Cf. Wevers, "Barthélemy and Proto-Septuagint Studies'' p. 29 and R. Hanhart, "Zum gegenwärtigen Stand der Septuagintaforschung''. In *De Septuaginta*, 3-19, p. 13 and ——, "An Early Revision of the Septuagint of Numbers''. In *Eretz-Israel 16. H.M. Orlinsky Volume*, Jerusalem 1982, p. 235*-239*, p. 238*.

no less exciting results. The coincidence of some Qumran readings, that differ from the *textus receptus*, with readings of the Septuagint[20] has made us very cautious in the interpretation of many Septuagint variant readings formerly attributed to the different translation techniques, when not to the incompetence of the translators[21]. Special mention should be made of those biblical books recovered in Qumran whose text differs from the *textus receptus* not only in some variant readings, but also from a literary point of view, while agreeing with the presumed Vorlage of the Septuagint: I refer to Samuel[a-c] and Jer[b] from Cave 4. The textual affiliation of 4QSam[a] with the *Vorlage* of the Septuagint is beyond doubt, thanks to the studies of Ulrich and Tov[22]. As far as Jeremiah is concerned, in spite of the scarcity of the fragments preserved, and the lack of a full edition, the fragments confirm the order and the strange disposition of Septuagint 10,5-10, in contrast with the *textus receptus*[23]. The repercussions of these new data for the text history of the Septuagint are far-reaching: not only the variant readings, but any change in the text of the Septuagint must be taken seriously, because theoretically these differences from the Masoretic text may go back to a different Hebrew text prior to the standardization of the 1st century A.D. In the case of Jeremiah, the Greek translator in all probability did not abbreviate the Hebrew text, as had been widely thought, but on the contrary it was the editor of the *textus receptus* who expanded a text very similar to the Vorlage of the Septuagint[24].

---

[20] Cf. 4QEx[a], 4QDeut[q], 4QJud[a], etc. In Ex. 1,5 4Q agrees with the Septuagint in the 75 descendants of Jacob against the 70 of the Masoretic Text. In the Song of Moses, concretely in Dt. 32,37-43, 4 Q witnesses to LXX readings supported by no Hebrew source previously known.

[21] Cf. P.W. Skehan, "A Fragment of the Song of Moses (Deut.32) from Qumran". *BASOR* 136 (1954) 12-15; J. Trebolle, "Textual Variants in 4QJudg[a] and the Textual and Editorial History of the Books of Judges". *RQ* 54,2 (1989) 229-245 and Fernández Marcos, "La Septuaginta y los hallazgos del Desierto de Judá", p. 237.

[22] Cf. E.Ch. Ulrich, *The Qumran Text of Samuel and Josephus*, Chico California 1978; E. Tov, "The Textual Affiliations of 4QSam[a]". *JSOT* 14 (1979) 37-53 and Fernández Marcos, "La Septuaginta y los hallazgos del Desierto de Judá", p. 238-239.

[23] Cf. Janzen *Studies in the Texts of Jeremiah*, Cambridge Mass. 1973, p. 182 and Fernández Marcos, "La Septuaginta y los hallazgos del Desierto de Judá", p. 240-241.

[24] Cf. Janzen, *Studies in the Texts of Jeremiah*, p. 10-17 and 135; P.-M. Bogaert, "*Urtext*, texte court et relecture: Jérémie XXXIII 14-26 TM et ses préparations". In *Congress Volume Leuven 1989*, edited by J.A. Emerton, Leiden 1991, p. 236-248.

Some authors think that a book like Samuel or Jeremiah constitutes the exception that confirms the rule, and that this cannot contradict the fact that most of the Septuagint books are translated from
a Vorlage very similar to the Masoretic text. Moreover, when the
early revisions of the Septuagint began to appear, they could have
been made using the Masoretic text as a criterion and trying to
accommodate the Greek to such a text[25]. On the contrary, no few
scholars maintain that in the light of Samuel and Jeremiah, one
must reckon on the possibility that other major disagreements between the Septuagint and the Hebrew may be due to a different
Vorlage of other books of the Septuagint, in spite of there not having
appeared until now any such Hebrew witnesses. Consequently a
different *Vorlage* has been postulated analogically for books like
Exodus 36-40 (Popper, Bogaert), Job (Orlinsky), Ezechiel (Lust,
Bogaert), Joshua (Orlinsky and recently Rofé), Judges (Trebolle),
Daniel (Jeansonne)[26].

In brief, thanks to the new evidence coming from the Judaean
Desert we are able to appreciate a fact that neither Origen nor Jerome
seem to have suspected, in spite of their both being well aware of the
big differences between the Septuagint and the current Hebrew text:
the Septuagint supports actual variants of the Hebrew, textual as
well as literary and, in some books at least, it is a witness to a textual
tradition different from the Masoretic one. Moreover, in the last
case, both traditions should be respected, and it is not permissible
from the point of view of the textual critic to accommodate one to
another[27]. This does not mean that we have to renounce a critical
restoration of the text closest to the original. Such an enterprise is
still valid provided the editor approaches to it with sound methods,
attending to all the witnesses, and avoiding any mixing of evidence
coming from heterogeneous sources. In some books, in the light of
the evidence recovered up to now, such a goal seems to lie far away

---

[25] For Hanhart the textual evidence in those books represent the exception that
confirms the rule of the unity of the Septuagint. But one can ask, is it the exception
or the rule, at least as soon as we leave the Pentateuch?

[26] Cf. E. Tov, *The Text-Critical Use of the Septuagint in Biblical Research*, Jerusalem
1981, p. 295-306; Sharon Pace Jeansonne, *The Old Greek Translation of Daniel 7-12*,
Washington 1988, p. 131-133 and H.M. Orlinsky, "The Septuagint and its Hebrew
Text". In *The Cambridge History of Judaism vol. II. The Hellenistic Age*, Cambridge
1989, 534-563, p. 559.

[27] I am referring to the treatment given to the LXX in some books of the *Biblia
Hebraica Stuttgartensia*, cf. Fernández Marcos, "The Use of the Septuagint" p. 69.

and perhaps will be unattainable[28]. For the time being it would be more convenient to respect the integrity of each tradition in a parallel or synoptic edition: the *textus receptus* on the one hand and the Septuagint on the other, as a witness to an *Hebraica veritas* that has disappeared or has been only preserved in fragments in Hebrew.

Over a century has gone by since P. de Lagarde, following Jerome's statement on the threefold division of the Septuagint tradition (in his famous Preface to Chronicles), edited the presumed Lucianic recension of the Greek Bible from Genesis to Esther[29], as a provisional step to restoring the *Ur-Septuaginta*. His ultimate goal was eventually to find the original translation, the Archetype, just as in the realm of the Hebrew, the search for the Archetype was the aim proposed in contemporaneous text criticism[30]. It was a pity, as his pupil Rahlfs pointed out, that such an important enterprise, based on a correct intuition, was carried out hurriedly and deficiently. In fact Rahlfs calls Lagarde's edition his biggest failure[31]. Nowadays we have learnt that the text history of the Septuagint is more complex than Lagarde thought, not only with regard to the possibility of restoring the original Septuagint, but also with regard to the heterogeneity of the different books. As far as the first problem is concerned, Prof. Wevers, the editor of the Pentateuch in the *series maior* of Göttingen has modestly restated the purpose of his critical editions: to approach as close as possible to an original that more and more disappears over the horizon of textual criticism. And, with regard to the three major recensions alluded to by Jerome, he points out that the Lucianic recension has not emerged for the Pentateuch, and for Hesychius we lack the confirmation of the evidence too[32].

---

[28] In spite of some scholars claiming that Biblical text criticism should not differ basically from the classical criticism. Being it true, at the same time one has to reckon on the text formation and text transmission quite different from that of the classical literature.

[29] P. de Lagarde, *Librorum Veteris Testamenti Canonicorum Pars Prior Graece*, Göttingen 1883.

[30] Cf. M.H. Goshen-Gottstein, "Hebrew Biblical Manuscripts". *Bib* 48 (1967) 243-290, p. 256-259. See also B. Chiesa, "Appunti di storia della critica del testo dell' Antico Testamento ebraico". *Henoch* XII, 1 (1990) 3-15, p. 4-5.

[31] Rahlfs informs critically about the strange procedure used by Lagarde in the preparation of this edition: "Diese Ausgabe des Lukiantextes ist überhaupt wohl der grösste Fehlschlag Lagardes", cf. A. Rahlfs, *Paul de Lagardes wissenschaftliches Lebenswerk*, Göttingen 1918, 78-79. See also *ibid.*, p. 74-79.

[32] Cf. John W. Wevers, "Barthélemy and Proto-Septuagint Studies", p. 27 and p. 30: "In fact, even for two of the three Christian recensions I can find no

If we turn now to consideration of the Hebrew Bible the material leads us back, in part, to the 3rd century B.C., and we have learned that at that time various textual traditions existed side by side, some more or less similar to the Masoretic Text—a kind of proto-Masoretic tradition—some nearer to the LXX (Old Greek or Hexaplaric), some nearer to the Samaritan Pentateuch tradition[33], the three major witnesses of the Pentateuch until 1947, called by Kahle "Haupttypen des Pentateuchtextes"[34]. The question now arises whether this threefold point of reference should be maintained when describing the manuscripts of the Judaean Desert, or whether a new hypothesis is preferable, calling for a larger fluidity of the text, inasmuch as it appears more close to the evidence. It is also plausible that many texts have disappeared, lacking the support of a community that considered them official or canonical, and therefore cared for their transmission[35].

We have started our edition of the Antiochene text of the Greek Bible with Samuel, as a result of many earlier preparatory studies and research. We have also learnt that the text history of the Septuagint cannot be treated as a whole. On the contrary, each book has its own history. Consequently, as it is well known, the so called Lucianic manuscripts begin to be Lucianic only in Ruth 4,11. Moreover, for the rest of the Octateuch we have not found any group of manuscripts that can be characterised as Lucianic or Antiochene, neither on the external criteria (quotations of the Antiochene Fathers) nor on the internal evidence (distinctive features of this recension)[36].

Our purpose has been to restore a text current in Antioch in the

---

convincing evidence", and ——, "Theodoret's *Quaest* and the Byzantine Text". *Henoch* 13 (1991) 29-64.

[33] Cf. M.H. Goshen-Gottstein, "The Hebrew Bible in the Light of the Qumran Scrolls and the Hebrew University Bible". *VTS* XL (1988) 42-53, p. 51.

[34] P. Kahle, "Untersuchungen zur Geschichte des Pentateuchtextes". *TSK* 88 (1915), 399-439 = *Opera Minora* (Leiden 1956) 3-37, p. 34.

[35] Cf. S. Talmon, "The Old Testament Text". In *The Cambridge History of the Bible. From the Beginnings to Jerome*, ed. P.R. Ackroyd and C.F. Evans, Cambridge 1970, 159-199, p. 198; and E. Tov, "Determining the Relationship between the Qumran Scrolls and the LXX". In *The Hebrew and Greek Texts of Samuel* ed. E. Tov Jerusalem 1980, p. 54-69.

[36] N. Fernández Marcos, "Some Reflections on the Antiochian Text of the Septuagint". In *Studien zur Septuaginta-Robert Hanhart zu Ehren. Aus Anlass seines 65. Geburtstages*, ed. D. Fraenkel, U. Quast and J.W. Wevers, Göttingen 1990, p. 219-229.

IV-V centuries A.D. Therefore it is an edited text, a revised text representing a particular stage in the text history of the Septuagint. Indeed this text is quite uniform for the historical books, and it has escaped the *kaige*-revision in Samuel-Kings. But it cannot be identified with the Old Greek because it has itself suffered at least some kind of stylistic revision, and very probably some pre-hexaplaric correction in accordance with the Hebrew. It is, in our opinion, an important step towards the restoration of the text closest to the Old Greek in Samuel-Kings. We also maintain (basically in agreement with Lagarde's theoretical programm) that the Greek text in the historical books still needs more minute discussion before a full critical edition can be carried out. As a matter of fact, an investigation into the translation technique of the Old Greek in the historical books would help to the text critical restoration, but again how is it possible to carry it out without knowing first where are the most faithful witnesses of the Old Greek?

Finally, this text cannot be considered to be only an instrument to restore the Old Greek, and eventually to improve the *textus receptus*. It has a value of its own, as the Septuagint known and read by a good deal of Christian Antiquity. Moreover, it is well known that the Antiochene text includes very ancient readings supported in the Historical books by the *Vetus Latina* and Josephus, and that some of these variant readings have an echo in the Qumran texts and in the Medieval Hebrew manuscripts[37]. Consequently, some of these readings, and many of its numerous double readings, are witnesses to variants and alternative readings going back to the stage of textual fluidity prior to the standardization of the Hebrew. In this perspective the Antiochene text may contribute to the present discussion on textual pluralism in the historical books[38].

---

[37] Cf. E.Ch. Ulrich, *The Qumran Text of Samuel and Josephus*; John W. Wevers, "A Study in the Hebrew Variants in the Books of Kings". *ZAW* 61 (1945-48) 43-76, p. 74-75, and A. Catastini, *Isaia ed Ezechia. Studio di storia della tradizione di II Re 18-20//Is 36-39*, Roma 1989, p. 243-255.

[38] See Hanhart's statement about the mass of ancient readings of the Antiochene recension, usually called Proto-Lucianic text: "Das Kriterium, nach welchem in früheren Zeiten eine solche Textform postuliert wurde: die Übereinstimmung von Textelemente, die in den Schriften der christlichen antiochenischen Exegetenschule überliefert sind, vor allem mit dem Text des Josephus und der Vetus Latina, ist durch die Bibeltexte von Qumran nur insofern präzisiert, als ihr Übereinstimmung in hebräischer Tradition heute als gesichert gelten darf", cf. R. Hanhart, "Zum gegenwärtigen Stand der Septuagintaforschung" p. 11.

I think that textual criticism today faces new challenges as a result of the progress achieved in the text history of the Bible around the Common Era. No longer can we pretend 1) to correct the Septuagint, in order to accommodate it anachronistically to the Hebrew *textus receptus* (like Origen), or 2) to disregard it in search of a more accurate translation (as made by the "three" younger translators and Jerome), or 3) to recur to tradition by declaring the Septuagint inspired and consqeuently literary independent of the original forgetting its status of translation (like Philo or Augustine). There is a fourth way: to edit the Septuagint critically, to maintain its integrity as a witness to *an Hebraica veritas*, at times the only witness to *the Hebraica veritas*, and to a text different from the *textus receptus*. As a Jewish translation it bears witness to *an Hebraica veritas* that, in some books should be considered synoptically, as a different redaction of the narrative. Hebrew and Greek texts together constitute τὰ βιβλία, because the *Hebraica veritas* was not unique and indivisible as Jerome thought (seduced by the phenomenon of the standardization of the consonantal text) but was represented, at the time of the translation, by different text traditions.[39]

In brief, Kahle postulated a plurality of translations into Greek. Nowadays scholars are more and more convinced that there was a plurality of text traditions in Hebrew at the time of the translation into Greek. In other words, the emphasis has shifted from the plurality of translations to the plurality of texts in the Hebrew *Vorlage*.

---

[39] In Late Antiquity the contemporary debate on the received Scriptures was certainly concerned with the books but not apparently with the different texts of these books. However the scribes were well aware of the text differences among the diverse manuscripts.

CHAPTER TWO

THE DIVERSE TEXTS OF THE SEPTUAGINT AND THE PROBLEMS OF AN EDITION

The study of the early history of the Septuagint has been carried on during this century under the influence of a polemic: that between Lagarde (with his pupils and heirs in Göttingen and elsewhere) on the one side, and Kahle with his pupils on the other. It can be said that every new witness of the Proto-Septuagint discovered in this period has been interpreted against the background of these two theories[1]. The basic correctness of Lagarde's intuition has been confirmed in its main lines, as the new evidence, on which Kahle supported his position, has been duly stratified in the text history of each book of the Septuagint. Thus Fouad Pap. 266 (1st century B.C.) and Rylands Pap. 458 (2nd century B.C.) belong to specific groups of manuscripts in the text history of Deuteronomy, as Wevers' critical edition of this book has shown[2]. The Greek fragments of Leviticus, Numbers and Deuteronomy from the Cave 4 of Qumran, as well as the fragments of Exodus and the Epistle of Jeremiah from Cave 7, witness also to a revised Septuagint, but not to a different translation[3]. Concerning the fragments of *Dodekapropheton* from Naḥal Ḥever, on which Kahle relied with renewed emphasis[4], Barthélemy's interpretation of them as a revision of the Old Septuagint according to the exegetical rules of the Palestinian Rabbinate has been generally admitted[5]. This perspective has not

---

[1] Cf. N. Fernández Marcos, *Introducción a las versiones griegas de la Biblia*, Madrid 1979, p. 57-70.

[2] The first one, Fouad Pap. 266, is an important witness to the primitive text of Deuteronomy. Although fragmentary, it contains a substantial amount of text from Dt. 17,14-23-29, cf. John W. Wevers, *Text History of the Greek Deuteronomy*, Göttingen 1978, p. 64-86. Rylands Pap. 458 is very fragmentary but, it must be emphasized, it was copied only ca. 150 years after the time of the translation.

[3] Cf. E. Ulrich, "The Greek Manuscripts of the Pentateuch from Qumran", p. 82, and Wevers, "An Early Revision of the Septuagint of Numbers", p. 235*-239*.

[4] P. Kahle, "Die Lederrolle mit dem griechischen Text der Kleinen Propheten und das Problem der LXX". *TLZ* 79 (1954) 81-94 (= *Opera Minora* (Leiden 1956) p. 113-127).

[5] Cf. John W. Wevers, "LXX-Forschungen seit 1954". *TR nF* 33 (1968) 18-76

changed with the publication of the long awaited diplomatic edition
and full study by Tov-Kraft-Parsons[6]. As far as Proto-Lucian is
concerned it should be stressed that some of the Pre-Lucianic witnesses mentioned by Metzger thirty years ago have been seriously
questioned in recent publications[7]. These conclusions are important because a Proto-Lucianic text counted as one of the various
translations on which Kahle relied for his Targumic explanation of
the origins of the Septuagint. As is well known, this presumed new
version was supposed to have constituted the base for Lucian's revision in the 4th century A.D.[8].

Kahle proposed the existence of another Greek translation in
Ephesus, relying on the evidence generally included under the sigla
of *Ur-Theodotion*. This translation would have been the base for the
revision of Theodotion in the 2nd century A.D. But in the light of
the new evidence, especially that of the fragments of Dodekapropheton, and the accurate study of the Pre-Hexaplaric Septuagint, the
hypothesis of various translations has been replaced by one of various early revisions, made according to the Hebrew texts (mainly the
Pre-Masoretic one) and other stylistic criteria.

It must be said clearly that research in the last decades has ad-
vanced along the lines of Lagarde's hypothesis. In other words, the
new evidence fits better in such a framework, and is better explained

and ———, "Proto-Septuagint studies". In *The Seed of Wisdom; Fs. T.J. Meek*,
Toronto 1964, 58-77, p. 77.

[6] Cf. *The Greek Minor Prophets Scroll From Naḥal Ḥever (8 ḤevXIIgr) (The Seiyâl Collection)*, by Emanuel Tov with the collaboration of R.A. Kraft and a contribution
by P.J. Parsons, Oxford 1990. The date of the Scroll, preferably 1st century B.C.,
adds a new dificulty to Barthélemy's identification of the reviser with Jonathan ben
Uzziel (ca. 30-50 A.D.), cf. D. Barthélemy, *Les Devanciers d'Aquila*, p. 149.

[7] For instance the Lucianic character of Rylands Pap. 458 to Deuteronomy or
Pap. 2054 to the Psalms in B.M. Metzger, "The Lucianic Recension of the Greek
Bible". *Chapters in the History of New Testament Textual Criticism (NTTS 4)*, Leiden
1963, 1-41. As far as Deuteronomy is concerned no Lucianic recension has been
detected up to now and the Lucianic text of the Psalter should be called more prop-
erly Byzantine text, cf. John W. Wevers, "Theodoret's *Quaest* and the Byzantine
Text". *Henoch* 13 (1991) 29-64; A. Pietersma, "Proto-Lucian and the Greek
Psalter". *VT* 28,1 (1978) 66-72, L.J. Perkins, "The So-called 'L' Text of Salms
72-82". *BIOSCS* 11 (1978) 44-63 and N. Fernández Marcos, "Some Reflections
on the Antiochian Text of the Septuagint". In *Studien zur Septuaginta—Robert Hanhart
zu Ehren*, herausgegeben von D. Fraenkel, U. Quast und J.W. Wevers, Göttingen
1990, 219-229, p. 221.

[8] P. Kahle, *Die Kairoer Geniza*, 271: "Eine solche frühere griechische Übersetzung scheint der Bibeltext gewesen zu sein, der in Antiochien entstanden und weit-
hin verbreitet war".

within a text history that relies on the original unity of the Septuagint translation rather than relying on a Targumic-like plurality of translations not attested anywhere up to now[9]. Even some cases of double texts, such as those of Judges, which according to Kahle represented a patent case of two different translations transmitted by mss. A and B[10], have been given a different explanation after the most recent systematic studies. All the salient differences can be integrated in a coherent process of revision, that is, the *kaige*-revision for the family of B and the Hexaplaric revision for the family of A, while the Lucianic group, especially when it agrees with the Vetus Latina, turns out to be the best witness for the Old Greek[11].

But at the same time it is necessary to emphasize that this basic assertion of the original unity of the translation has to be toned down in multiple aspects. This unity cannot be conceived in the same way for the Pentateuch as for the rest of the Septuagint. The Pentateuch, as it is well known, was the only part of the Septuagint alluded to in the Letter of Aristeas, and it has been used as a lexicon for the later translations of other books[12]. Besides, there is the reality of different translators for the different books or groups of books, and the fact that the rest of the Biblical literature outside the Pentateuch was never treated in Jewish circles with the same respect as the Torah, in spite of being recognized as normative already in the Prologue of Ben Sira (ca. 116 B.C.). Moreover, for the time being even in the books of the Torah, not every problem concerning the early history of the Septuagint has been solved. We can mention, for in-

---

[9] This was Kahle's model, cf. P. Kahle, *Die Kairoer Geniza*, 260-261. We leave aside the evidence coming from Philo's quotations as support for his theory, a prove already abandoned by his pupil Katz, cf. P. Katz, *Philo's Bible*, Cambridge 1950. On the So-called 'Bible of the Apostles' applied to the quotations of the New Testament that differ from the text of Codex Vaticanus, see N. Fernández Marcos, "La Biblia de los autores del Nuevo Testamento". In *II Simposio Bíblico Español*, ed. V. Collado Bertomeu and V. Vilar Hueso, Valencia-Córdoba 1987, p. 171-180.

[10] P. Kahle, *Die Kairoer Geniza*, 249 and ——, *The Cairo Geniza*, Oxford 1959, p. 236: "Whoever is acquainted with conditions prevailing in older Targums at a time before an autoritative text was fixed, will recognize in these two Greek texts examples of two forms of an Old Targum".

[11] Cf. Walter R. Bodine, *The Greek Text of Judges. Recensional Developments*, HSM 23, Chico California 1980, p. 134-136 and 186.

[12] Cf. I.L. Seeligmann, *The Septuagint Version of Isaiah. A Discussion of its Problems*, Leiden 1948, p. 44-49; G. Gerleman, *Studies in the Septuagint II. Chronicles*, Lund 1946, p. 22-30 and E. Tov, "The Impact of the LXX Translation of the Pentateuch on the Translation of the other Books". In *Mélanges Dominique Barthélemy*, ed. by P. Casetti, O. Keel and A. Schenker, Fribourg/Göttingen 1981, 577-593.

stance, the final chapters of Exodus 36-40 or the final verses of
Joshua if we consider the Octateuch[13]. Besides, new data introduce
elements of discord in the harmonious version of our presumed
reconstructions. The so-called Pentateuchal Paraphrasis in some
unedited fragments of Qumran may be related with such phenomena of expansions in the Vorlage of the Septuagint or the *Vetus
Latina*[14]. I wonder why Kahle hardly mentions in passing the *Vetus
Latina*, in spite of its being a secondary version so close to the Septuagint that it could provide more arguments for his hypothesis of a
plurality of texts and translations[15], as we will try to show in our next
chapters.

It may be that the cases on which I am going to focus now represent the "exception that proves the rule" with regard to the unity
of the translation, using Hanhart's words[16]. Nevertheless it is worth
reflecting on them as a part of the Septuagint tradition that stub-
bornly escapes our more or less brilliant theories.

When we leave the realm of the Pentateuch and the Later Prophets—just the books already edited in the Göttingen *series maior*—we
realise that the text history of the Septuagint becomes more and
more complicated, and even whithin those books we have already
noticed that in the final chapters of Exodus, the Septuagint and
probable the *Vetus Latina* bear witness to a Hebrew Vorlage different
from the *textus receptus*[17]. I leave aside at this point the apparent signs
of different redactions detected in the books of Jeremiah, Samuel-
Kings and Ezechiel[18]. In fact, these cases do not affect so much the

---

[13] Cf. D.W. Gooding, *The Account of the Tabernacle. Translation and Textual Problems of the Greek Exodus*, Cambridge 1959 and D. Fraenkel, "Die Quellen der asteri-
sierten Zusätze im zweiten Tabernakelbericht Exod 35-40". In *Studien zur Septuaginta—Robert Hanhart zu Ehren*, p. 140-187. A. Rofé, "The End of the Book of
Joshua According to the Septuagint". *Henoch* 4 (1982) 17-36. According to Rofé
the Septuagint reflects, for Jos 24,33a-b, an autonomous Hebrew text whose existence is witnessed by the *Damascus Document* V, 1-5.

[14] Cf. E. Tov, "The Textual Status of 4Q364-367 (4QPP)". *In The Madrid
Qumran Congress. Proceedings of the International Congress on the Dead Sea Scrolls, Madrid
18-21 March 1991. Edited by* Julio Trebolle Barrera & Luis Vegas Montaner,
Volume One, Madrid/Leiden 1992, p. 43-83.

[15] On the Hebraisms of the Coptic Versions cf. P. Kahle, *Die Kairoer Genisa*,
p. 272.

[16] Cf. R. Hanhart, "Zum gegenwärtigen Stand der Septuagintaforschung",
p. 9.

[17] Cf. P.-M. Bogaert, in *La Bible d'Alexandrie. 2 L'Exode* par A. Le Boulluec et
P. Sandevoir, Paris 1989, 61-67 p. 66.

[18] Cf. J.G. Janzen, *Studies in the Text of Jeremiah*, Cambridge Mass. 1973 and

postulate of the unity of the translation, but rather that of the unity of the Hebrew text underlying the Septuagint as compared with the Masoretic Text.

I will examine now some examples of double or threefold texts, edited and recognised as such by the editors of the Septuagint Unternehmen in Göttingen. For the book of Tobit, the editor, R. Hanhart, has found that the Greek tradition of the book has been transmitted in two, and partially in three, different textforms. In view of the agreements among them some kind of textual connection has to be supposed. But despite this mutual dependence, the disagreements are so deep and multiple that they cannot be due merely to the work of recension, but must be designated as autonomous textforms[19]. The *Vetus Latina* follows the expanded text of *Codex Sinaiticus*, but it attests also several disagreements from it which cannot be attributed to free translation, but must go back to a different Greek *Vorlage* attested by the ms. 319[20]. Just because the Tobit tradition lacks unity and homogeneity, and because many intermediate links in the transmission fail, Hanhart renounces to restore the original text of that book[21].

The case of Esther is also illuminating. Hanhart edits both textforms (the so called Septuagint-text(o') and the L'-text) separately, realising that the L'-text represents a re-elaboration of the Septuagint-text based on older Esther traditions. By means of a set of linguistic criteria Hanhart is able to establish the priority of the Septuagint-text in relation to the L'-text[22]. Interestingly enough the L'-text

---

E. Tov, *The Septuagint Translation of Jeremiah and Baruch*, Missoula Mont.1975. E. Tov (ed.), *The Hebrew and Greek Texts of Samuel*, Jerusalem 1980. J. Lust (ed.), *Ezechiel and his Book. Textual and Literary Criticism and their Interrelation*, Leuven 1986.

[19] Cf. R. Hanhart, *Text und Textgeschichte des Buches Tobit*, Göttingen 1983, p. 11: "Der griechische Text ist in zwei, zum Teil in drei Textformen überliefert, deren teilweise Übereinstimmungen zwar dermassen eindeutig sind, dass gegenseitige Abhängigkeit mit Sicherheit angenommen werden muss, deren Urterschiede aber so tiefgreifend sind, dass ihr Verhältnis zueinander nicht als Rezension sondern als selbständige Textform bestimmt werden muss".

[20] Hanhart, *Text und Textgeschichte des Buches Tobit*, p. 12.

[21] Commenting the contribution of the *Vetus Latina* to the reconstruction of Tobit Hanhart points out: "dass der zukünftige Kommentator des Buches Tobit in der altlateinischen Übersetzung den Schlüssel für die Lösung mancher Probleme finden wird, die es ihm, unter Verzicht auf die Reconstruktion eines Urtextes, ermöglichen, der Feststellung der ältesten Tobitüberlieferung näherzukommen" *ibid.* p. 17.

[22] R. Hanhart, *Septuaginta. Vetus Testamentum Graecum. VIII/5 Esther*, Göttingen 1966, p. 89-90. Cf. E. Tov, "The 'Lucianic' Text of the Canonical and Apocryphal

cannot be identified with either the Lucianic or with the Proto-Lucianic recension[23], as had been thought in the past.

According to Hanhart other elaborations of the Greek tradition of Esther appear very early next to the Septuagint-text: first of all the L'-text that includes the whole book. Secondly, the Greek Vorlage of the *Vetus Latina*. Rests of another rearrangement can be detected in the text used by Josephus[24]. Admittedly Hanhart concludes that, as none of these textforms can be explained independently of the Septuagint-text, in fact all of them point to the basic unity of the Greek Esther[25]. But at least one has to admit that the disagreements among these text traditions is so strong that they cannot be connected in any stemmatic relation and consequently they are best edited in a parallel or synoptic form[26].

Daniel is a third book that has been edited in the Göttingen *series maior* in a double, parallel text: the θ'-text, traditionally attributed to Theodotion and transmitted by the majority of the manuscript tradition, and the Septuagint-text, very rarely attested by the ms. 88 and the *Syrohexapla* in its Hexaplaric form and by Pap. 967 in its Pre-Hexaplaric stage. The relationship between both texts has not been satisfactorily explained up to now[27]. As in other books of the Septu-

---

Sections of Esther: A Rewritten Biblical Book''. *Textus* 10 (1982) 1-25 and J.-C. Haelewyck, ''Le texte dit 'Lucianique' du livre d'Esther. Son étendue et sa cohérence''. *Le Muséon* 98,1-2 (1985) 5-45, p. 42: ''A partir de l'original hébreu une première version grecque fut realisée qui constitue le modèle grec de la *Vetus Latina*''.

[23] Hanhart, *Esther*, p. 92-95.

[24] Hanhart, *Esther*, p. 96.

[25] Hanhart, *Esther*, p. 99: ''Die aus dem 'L-Text' der altlat. Überlieferung und Josephus bruchstückhaft erkennbare Existenz weiterer griechischer Textformen neben dem o'-Text ist aber—da keine dieser Textformen unabhängig vom o'-Text erklärbar ist—, trotz ihrer Mannigfaltigkeit ein Beweis nicht gegen, sondern für die Existenz eines einheitlichen, algemein anerkannten und verbreiteten griechischen Grundtextes des Est-Buches''.

[26] Cf. J.T. Milik, ''Les modèles araméens du livre d'Esther dans la Grotte 4 de Qumrân''. *RQ* 15,3 (1992) (*Mémorial Jean Starcky*) 321-399, p. 389: ''L'histoire des versions grecques du livre d'*Esther* commence paradoxalement par des textes Vieux Latins d'origine ouest-africaine, dont les témoins préservés de nos jours sont cités au début de ce mémoire'', and p. 398: ''Si l'on accepte notre esquisse d'histoire des textes grecs d'*Esther*, il n'y eut pas de place pour des originaux araméens ou hébreux ni au début, lors de la composition du texte grec sous-jacent à la VL, ni à la fin, au moment du travail entrepris par Lysimaque fils de Ptolémée''.

[27] N. Fernández Marcos, *Introducción a las versiones griegas de la Biblia*, p. 74-76. For Di Lella, ''Theodotion-Daniel is a fresh translation of the Hebrew and Aramaic form of the book with an eye on LXX-Daniel'', cf. A.A. Di Lella, *The Book of Daniel*, The Anchor Bible 23, New York 1978, p. 82.

agint it seems that the Septuagint-translation may be considered more free than the θ'-text, and not governed by a tendentious approach or by a concrete theological interpretation[28].

The restoration of the Greek Sira presented a different problem. The editor, J. Ziegler, adopted a new procedure—using different characters in printing—in order to keep the identity of the two Greek forms (GI and GII) separate. In his opinion they do not reflect two independent translations, but GII used GI and in addition translated anew where he thought it was necessary. In any case Ziegler shares the opinion that different translations of Ben Sira were in existence, at least for the first part of the book. They would have arisen as soon as it was realised that the first version did not agree with the Hebrew. Let us remember the feeling of the first translator (as echoed in the words of the Prologue) that even the most accurate translation lacks the force of the original[29]. These diverse versions have left traces in the recensions of Lucian and Origen and above all in the *Vetus Latina*[30]. It is worth noting in passing that these words of the Göttingen editor would be strongly supported by Kahle. Likewise Wevers emphasizes that GII is certainly older than the New Testament, since Sir 48,10c has been quoted by Luke 1,17[31]. Thiele's recent edition of the *Vetus Latina* of Ben Sira has shed some

---

[28] Cf. Sharon P. Jeansonne, *The Old Greek Translation of Daniel 7-12*, Washington 1988, p. 131-133; P.-M. Bogaert, "Relecture et refonte historicisantes du livre de Daniel attestées par la première version grecque (Papyrus 967)". In *Études dur le judaïsme hellénistique*, ed. by R. Kunzmann and J. Schlosser, Paris 1984, 197-224; ———, "Le témoignage de la Vetus Latina dans l'étude de la tradition des Septante. Ézéchiel et Daniel dans le papyrus 967". *Bib* 59 (1978) 384-395, and E. Ulrich, "Daniel Manuscripts from Qumran. Part 1: A Preliminary Edition of 4QDanᵃ". *BASOR* 268 (1987) 17-37; ———, "Daniel Manuscripts from Qumran. Part 2: Preliminary Editions of 4QDanᵇ and 4QDanᶜ". *BASOR* 274 (1989) 3-26.

[29] Cf. J. Ziegler, *Septuaginta. Vetus Testamentum Graecum. XII/2 Sapientia Iesu Filii Sirach*, Göttingen 1965, p. 125: οὐ γὰρ ἰσοδυναμεῖ αὐτὰ ἐν ἑαυτοῖς Ἑβραιστὶ λεγόμενα καὶ ὅταν μεταχθῇ εἰς ἑτέραν γλῶσσαν· οὐ μόνον δὲ ταῦτα, ἀλλὰ καὶ αὐτὸς ὁ νόμος καὶ αἱ προφητεῖαι καὶ τὰ λοιπὰ τῶν βιβλίων οὐ μικρὰν ἔχει διαφορὰν ἐν ἑαυτοῖς λεγόμενα.

[30] Ziegler, *Sapientia Iesu Filii Sirach*, p. 74: "So ist es auch nicht richtig, von nur einer zweiten griech. Übersetzung zu sprechen, sondern es ist anzunehmen, dass mehrere griech. Übersetzungen im Umlauf waren, von denen uns namentlich im ersten Teil des Buches ziemlich umfangreiche Überreste in der OL-Rezension und vor allem in La überliefert sind".

[31] Wevers, "Septuaginta-Forschungen seit 1954", p. 42. Compare Luke 1,17: ἐπιστρέψαι καρδίαν πατέρων ἐπὶ τέκνα with Ben Sira 48,10c: ἐπιστρέψαι καρδίαν πατρὸς πρὸς υἱόν with variants.

light on this textual problem, but his cautious statements have not
clarified the relationship between the diverse textual forms of the
book. On one hand he emphasizes some parallels between the *Vetus
Latina* of Ben Sira and the Western text of the New Testament[32]; on
the other, he compares the relation between the textual form of the
Greek Proverbs and the Hebrew text with the relation between the
Vetus Latina of Ben Sira and the Greek tradition[33]. But both examples attempt to explain the unknown by the less known and leave
us in a kind of permanent perplexity. At the same time he realises
that a high proportion of the doublets do not come from the process
of text transmission, but belong to the original translation, and he
wonders at which stage of the Greek tradition (between GI and GII)
the Greek Vorlage of the Vetus Latina should be inserted[34].

Up to now we have considered the policy of the Göttingen school
in the edition of books whose textual tradition splits drastically from
a very early time into two or more branches. We can mention in
passing other books, like Proverbs or Samuel-Kings, the critical edition of which is still awaited; in all probability they will torture their
future editors with similar problems.

In spite of this complex panorama perhaps it is possible and convenient to draw some general conclusions that will help to set in a
new light the ancient Lagarde-Kahle polemic, that has dominated
the discussion of the main Septuagint problems almost during one
century.

Extant remains of different Greek translations of a definite book
of the Septuagint without connection with each other still remain in
the realm of fancy. Therefore it must be stressed that Lagarde was
right about the fundamental unity of the origins of the Septuagint.
But at the same time it has been established through the new data
from Qumran and other textual studies of the last decades that:
a) recensional activity on the original Septuagint began so early that
in some cases it almost coincided with the first appearance of the
translation. Traces have been detected of many Pre-Hexaplaric
revisions in accordance with the Hebrew, though not as consistent
as in Origen's recension[35]; b) moreover, in several books different

---

[32] W. Thiele, *Vetus Latina 11/2 Sirach (Ecclesiasticus)*, Freiburg 1988, p. 102 n. 1.
[33] Thiele, *Sirach*, p. 112.
[34] Thiele, *Sirach*, p. 110.
[35] Cf. P. Katz in *Studia Patristica vol. I (= TU 63)*, Berlin 1957, p. 346-348. See
also P. Katz in *ZAW* 69 (1957), p. 78-80 and notes 2 and 3.

kinds of textual elaboration and rearrangement have occurred that preclude any attempt to restore an original text, not to speak of the confusion created by the irruption of Christian recensions, especially the Hexaplaric.

It seems too that the diverse treatment accorded to the different books in the first stage of their text transmission, as well as in the period of the great recensions, is closely connected with the status that each book had achieved in the process of canonization[36]. This statement finds confirmation if we turn our attention to the textual fluidity detected in many pseudepigraphic writings as *The Testament of Abraham*, transmitted in a double redaction, *The Testaments of the Twelve Patriarchs* or *The Lives of the Prophets* with a short and long recension[37].

Consequently, the frontier between "translation technique" on the first level of approach to the language of the original and "recensional activity", that very often uses accommodation to the original as its main criterion, becomes more and more difficult to establish. In fact these circumstances have brought forth for some books several textual forms that cannot be reduced stemmatically to a single text, nor stratified chronologically in a sequence of coherent recensions. That is the reason why nowadays the ancient opposition between representatives of the two opposite theories, those of Lagarde and Kahle, has been subjected to a progressive relativization. In a sense the Targum hypothesis presupposes a unification of possible co-existing translations, while the hypothesis of unity admits the postulate of different translators for different books, and even within a single book, as well as constant revisions and occasional re-elaborations that produced a plurality of text forms. Both phenomena do not contradict the original unity of the Septuagint but in

---

[36] Fernández Marcos, "Some Reflections on the Antiochian Text of the Septuagint", p. 226-227.

[37] Cf. M. Delcor, *Le Testament d' Abraham*, Leiden 1973, p. 5: "Le fond seul est commun aux deux narrations; chacun d'elles a sa rédaction propre, celui des deux auteurs qui aurait abrégé ou amplifié le récit de l'autre n'a pas fait oeuvre de plagiat", and F. Schmidt, *Le Testament grec d' Abraham*, Tübingen 1986. M. de Jonge (ed.), *Studies on the Testament of the Twelve Patriarchs*, Leiden 1975, p. 45-87; H.W. Hollander and M de Jonge, *The Testaments of the Twelve Patriarchs. A Commentary*, Leiden 1985 and M. de Jonge, *The Testaments of the Twelve Patriarchs. A Critical Edition of the Greek Text*, Leiden 1978. On *The Lives of the Prophets* with a short and long recension cf. Th. Schermann, *Prophetarum Vitae Fabulosae, Indices apostolorum discipulorumque Domini*, Leipzig 1907, 1-106.

Hanhart's words, "die Art und Weise ihrer Entstehung und ihrer frühen Geschichte sind die Ursache dafür, dass die ursprüngliche Einheitlichkeit oft fast bis zur Unkenntlichkeit verschleiert ist"[38]. In fact nowadays the aim of the Göttingen editors has become more modest, merely trying to reach in their critical restoration a stage of language as near as possible to the original[39]; moreover, in some books even this modest goal cannot be maintained and the editor has to content himself with the restoration of two or three textual forms, as he is unable to go back to an earlier stage of the tradition[40].

We have seen that the sharp distinction between the supposed unity of the original Septuagint and the plurality due to the presumed Targumic origin of the translation has become blurred because of the early revisions, that tried to accommodate the first translation to the current Hebrew text. The impulse to recensional activity prevailed over the desire to preserve the original text in such a way that in time recension or updating dominated over preservation. On the other hand in several books different kind of reelaborations occurred, using material from diverse traditions. As a result of these phenomena in the text transmission the alternative between unity/plurality does not appears as final and exclusive as Kahle and Lagarde supposed.

At this point, as we saw in the previous lecture, a new factor emerges that complicates still more the textual panorama: as has been confirmed by the Qumran evidence, for some books of the OT, at the turn of the era there was a state of textual fluidity even at the level of the Hebrew[41]. Indeed this factor has contributed to

---

[38] Hanhart, "Zum gegenwärtigen Stand der Septuagintaforschung", p. 8.

[39] John W. Wevers, *Septuaginta. Vetus Testamentum Graecum. I Genesis*, Göttingen 1974, p. 63: "Es handelt sich bei dem hier vorgelegten kritischen Text um eine Annäherung an den LXX-Text, hoffentlich die beste, die aufgrund des gegenwärtigen Standes unserer Kenntnis rekonstruiert werden kann. Der Herausgeber unterliegt nicht der Illusion, dass er durchgängig den ursprünglichen Septuagintatext wiederhergestellt habe". For the book of Jeremiah Bogaert extends the difficulty to reach the original to the *Urtext*: "Dans cette étude en perspective de la croissance historique d'un recueil prophétique, menée à rebours, comme le fait l'arquéologue, à partir de l'état final, l'Urtext est le point de fuite ou, comme le dit si bien l'anglais, le *vanishing point*, à la fois nécessaire, réel et inaccessible", cf. P.-M. Bogaert, "*Urtext*, Texte court et Relecture", p. 247.

[40] Cf. Hanhart, *Esther*, p. 96-99 and —— *Tobit*, p. 31-36.

[41] The Biblical text was in such a way dominated by harmonization that it is difficult at times even to distinguish between Biblical text and Paraphrase. To these categories it should be added another one: the use of Biblical and Parabiblical

strengthen the relevance of the Septuagint translation. Many of the Septuagint deviations from the *textus receptus*, attributed by former generations of scholars to different translation techniques, or to the theological tendencies of the translators, have been shown to be due to the use of a different Hebrew Vorlage. Consequently, the Septuagint can be used as a witness to a different (and perhaps older) Hebrew text, and its tradition has to be respected as a witness to the textual pluralism at the level of the Hebrew itself[42].

On the other hand, important as the restoration of the original Septuagint may be, in the light of this new perspective (as a privileged witness of a different Hebrew text not fully preserved in the original language) it also becomes relativized in the framework of a textual pluralism that affects the state of the Hebrew Vorlage in the very period in which the Greek translation was being brought forth and during the first stage of its transmission. In other words, the search for the original Septuagint needs to be relieved of the theological component that involved textual criticism in former periods[43]. Just as the diversity of texts of the Synoptic Gospels has not affected the canonicity of the New Testament, the different texts for some books of the Old Testament should not be an obstacle to their canonicity[44]. The Old Greek need not be thought of any more as the necessary nexus with a hypothetical Hebrew Archetype, as Lagarde thought, but rather as a useful door to a lost Hebrew text. At this level the dialogue between textual criticism and literary criticism has already started, as can be appreciated from a set of synoptic studies that have taken into account the different texts of Samuel-Kings[45].

---

material to rewrite part of a book, a book or a section of the Bible. The permanent concern for updating the text makes Biblical transmission quiet different from the transmission of a classical work.

[42] Consequently one should not try to accommodate the Greek to the *textus receptus*. And this should make us very cautious too when using the Septuagint as an instrument to restore and improve the Masoretic text, a procedure that has been applied too often in successive editions of the *Biblia Hebraica*, cf. Fernández Marcos, "The Use of the Septuagint in the Criticism of the Hebrew Bible", p. 63-66.

[43] On the theological presuppositions underlying Lagarde's textual theory cf. M.H. Goshen-Gottstein, "Theory and Practice of Textual Criticism. The Text-Critical Use of the Septuagint". *Textus* 3 (1963) 130-159.

[44] Cf. J.A. Sanders, "Stability and Fluidity in Textual Canon". In *Tradition of the Text* ed. by G.J. Norton and S. Pisano, Freiburg/Göttingen 1991, 203-217, p. 216 note 48.

[45] Cf. E. Ulrich, "Horizons of Old Testament Textual Research at the Thirtieth Anniversary of Qumran Cave 4". *CBQ* 46,4 (1984) 613-636, p. 624 and p. 631.

In this respect perhaps the best tradition of our Polyglot Bibles (those of Alcalá, Antwerp, Paris and London) has something to teach us in this new trend of Biblical text criticism. They respected and edited in their integrity the different textual witnesses and by means of these one can compare synoptically the different textual traditions. All of them form part of the whole Bible, a collection of books, in reality a whole library (as was rightly understood in the Middle Ages). We hope that this will be seen now not only with reference to the plurality of books and literary genres, but also with reference to the plurality of texts and redactions detected in several of the books of the Septuagint[46].

---

[46] The double perspective of the text should be taken into account: the vertical or genetic one that tries to restore, if possible, the stage of text nearest to the original. This view should be completed with the horizontal or synoptic one that takes into account the different editions that co-exist and occasionally are simultaneously in circulation. The exegesis has to consider both aspects of the process of text transmission. But the text critic cannot renounce to establish the relationship among the different texts or redactions he finds in the manuscripts.

CHAPTER THREE

THE ANTIOCHENE TEXT OF THE GREEK BIBLE: A REVISED AND EDITED TEXT

As I started working in the early seventies on text criticism of the Greek Bible within the research programm of the Biblia Polyglota Matritensia, my first step was to contact Prof. Hanhart in Göttingen and Prof. Barthélemy in Fribourg. The Göttingen enterprise was advancing at a regular rhythm and its editions were warmly approved by the scientific world. I soon became aware that it would be nonsense to repeat unnecessarily the collation of manuscripts and further critical work. Therefore I thought it could be useful in the framework of our project to edit not the original Septuagint or the stage of language closest to the original, but a recension of the Greek Bible. This plan had two advantages: on the one hand it did not interfere with the Göttingen project and on the other it would lead to an edition that could be of some value for Patristics, students of Ancient Philology and the text history of the Septuagint self. Besides, some scholars had pointed out the need for an edition of this kind. In this context it is unevoidable to quote the final words of a short but accurate article by S. Brock that influenced decisively our project: "Indeed I should like to end by pointing out that Origen has something to teach the modern textual critic of the LXX: such a scholar, influenced by classical scholarship, exerts all his energy on recovering the original texts of the translators, forgetting that the LXX was a living and ever changing entity, and forgetting too that many scholars outside his own field—and here I have in mind the patristic scholar in particular—would like to see an edition of the LXX as current, say, in fourth century Antioch—to give one example that might actually be feasible—"[1].

Among the extant recensions preserved in the ancient sources I did not hesitate in the election. The Lucianic recension seemed to be the most worth editing for different reasons: 1) Lagarde's failure to produce it, in spite of the correctness of his principles; 2) the exis-

---

[1] Cf. S.P. Brock, "Origen's aims as a Textual Critic of the Old Testament", p. 218.

tence of an external criterion in the quotations of the Antiochene
Fathers; 3) the high quality of such a text for the historical books as
had been pointed out by Thenius, Wellhausen and Driver[2]; and
4), last but not least, the fact that the Polyglot of Alcalá had edited,
be it accidentally, a text of Lucianic character for the Historical
books. In addition the relevance of recent discussion of the Lucianic
and Proto-Lucianic texts and their connection with the Hebrew text
of 4QSam[a-c] could not be overlooked.

Since Lagarde's attempt to establish the Lucianic text of the Octateuch, new studies had been carried out with the aim of identifying
the genuine Lucianic text for every part of the Octateuch. The most
important contributions had come from the Göttingen school. First
of all Dahse recognized in the group of manuscripts *fir* of Brooke-
McLean's edition for Genesis those closest to the Lucianic recension. Then Hautsch did the same for the Octateuch, and Rahlfs for
the Historical books. Hautsch realised that the Lucianic manuscripts differ from book to book and he identified the minuscles
representative of this recension for each book of the Octateuch.
Rahlfs identified two new witnesses of the Lucianic recension for the
books of Kings and he produced a detailed and accurate study of this
recension in those books. But when he published his edition of Genesis (1926), he maintained against Hautsch that manuscript *75* of
Rahlfs' Catalogue was the best witness of the Lucianic text[3].

Faced with such uneven results I thought that one of the reasons
for the uncertainty concerning the Lucianic recension of the Octateuch was the lack of critical editions of the Antiochene Fathers.
Lagarde has used uncritical editions for the quotations of Chrysostom and subsequent scholars continued using Savile's and
Schulze's editions, both reprinted in Migne's *Patrologia Graeca*, for
Chrysostom and Theodoret respectively.

---

[2] Cf. M.H. Goshen-Gottstein, "The Book of Samuel—Hebrew and Greek—
Hindsight of a Century". *Textus* XIV (1988) 147-161.

[3] Cf. N. Fernández Marcos-A. Sáenz Badillos, *Theodoreti Cyrensis Quaestiones in
Octateuchum*, Madrid 1979, p. XXIX-XXXIX. A. Rahlfs, *Verzeichnis der griechischen
Handschriften des Alten Testaments*, Berlin 1914. In a survey on the project of the
Septuaginta-Unternehmen written by R. Smend in 1907 one can read on the edition of the Lucianic recension: "Die sogenannte Rezension des Lucian lässt sich
anscheinend in grossem Umfang rekonstruiren; ob in vollem, lässt sich zur Zeit noch
nich übersehen. Es ist deshalb fraglich, ob eine vollständige Ausgabe des Lucian
jemals möglich sein wird", cf. R. Smend, "Der geistige Vater des Septuaginta-
Unternehmen". In *Studien zur Septuaginta—Robert Hanhart zu Ehren*, 332-344, p. 336.

Consequently, I considered it unavoidable to first edit critically Theodoret's text, before using it as control of the Lucianic recension of the Octateuch. Thus we undertook the edition of Theodoret's *Quaestiones in Octateuchum*, a work in which Theodoret quotes a large part of the Octateuch and, in contrast with Chrysostom, does so quite literally. The critical restoration of Theodoret's text in relation to the study of the *catenae* was rightly emphasized by Francoise Petit from Leuven[4]. But the results for the study of the Biblical text were rather disappointing. There was no consistent group of manuscripts supporting Theodoret's text. This text, hardly defined at the beginning of the Pentateuch, became in Joshua-Judges-Ruth a little more characterized with distinctive features, but these were in no way comparable with the characteristics of this text in Samuel to Chronicles, or even in the Prophetic books[5].

In an article published in 1978 I have explained in detail the relation of Theodoret's biblical text with the different groups of manuscripts of the Septuagint for the Octateuch. There I show how the entity of this text, blurred at the beginning of the Octateuch becomes progressively more defined in the later books[6], where it can be better appreciated as the type of text followed by Theodoret. In Ruth, for instance, Theodoret agrees with the text of the manuscripts *glnowe₂* (plus *b* from Ruth 4,11 on) of Brooke-McLean's edition, and this type of text has already the main features of the Antiochene recension. In Judges we find traces of intentional, but inconsistent, stylistic revision. And, to a decreasing degree, traces of stylistic revision can be observed going back to Numbers. But these traces of slight stylistic revision do not substantiate the case for a Lucianic recension.

These conclusions, the result of our critical edition of Theodoret's *Quaestiones in Octateuchum*, have been confirmed, when the material of the tradition has been duly stratified, in the critical edition of the Greek Pentateuch carried out by Wevers[7].

---

[4] Cf. F. Petit, "La tradition de Théodoret de Cyr dans les chaînes sur la Genèse". *Le Muséon* 92,3-4 (1979) 281-286 and F. Petit, *Catenae graecae in genesim et in exodum, II. Collectio Coisliniana, In genesim* 1 vol., Turnhout 1986.

[5] Cf. N. Fernández Marcos, "Theodoret's Biblical Text in the Octateuch". *BIOSCS* 11 (1978) 27-43 and ——, "Some Reflections on the Antiochian Text of the Septuagint", p. 220-221.

[6] Fernández Marcos, "Theodoret's Biblical Text in the Octateuch", p. 39.

[7] John W. Wevers, "A Lucianic recension in Genesis?". *BIOSCS* 6 (1973) 22-35; ——, "The Göttingen Septuagint". *BIOSCS* 8 (1975) 19-23, p. 22 and ——,

As the case for a Lucianic recension of the Pentateuch and of other books of the Septuagint (like Esther or Psalms) gradually weakened—in Tobit no trace of a Lucianic recension has been found[8]—, the attention of scholars became focused more and more on Samuel-Kings. Three factors contributed to emphasize the importance of this recension for the Historical books: 1) The publication by Barthélemy of *Les Devanciers d'Aquila* (1963), according to which the Lucianic manuscripts for Samuel-Kings formed the only group that escaped the *kaige* revision along those books; 2) Brock's dissertation on the *Recensions of the Septuagint version of 1 Samuel* (Oxford 1966), establishing the recensional character of this text; and, 3) The discovery of the Qumran fragments of 4QSam[a-c] and the discussion that arose on the Proto-Lucianic text[9].

Stimulated by this new focus of interest, we extended our editorial work to Theodoret's *Quaestiones in Reges et Paralipomena*, this time with quite different results for the study of the Biblical text. According to our edition, the proportion of Theodoret's agreements with the Lucianic group of manuscripts is shown to be very high; the number of Theodoret's particular readings has been considerably reduced; and a good number of the new readings recovered follow the Lucianic manuscripts[10].

After this long preparatory work we could start the edition of the Antiochene text on a more reliable basis, if only for Samuel-Kings-

---

Text History of the Greek Genesis, Göttingen 1974, p. 175: "Only one conclusion is possible on the basis of the actual textual evidence, namely that if Lucian made a recension of Genesis it was not used by Chr/Tht, nor to the best of our knowledge is it anywhere extant". Cf. now, after completing the edition of the whole Pentateuch in Greek, the results of his research in J.W. Wevers, "Theodoret's *Quaest* and the Byzantine Text", p. 37: "But these statistics in no way solve the vexed problem of Lucian in the Pentateuch; they only show that if Lucian revised the Pentateuch its traces must be sought in the Byzantine text. What gives one pause, however, is that there is next to no trace in these lists of any of the characteristics commonly attributed to Lucian... One must conclude that the evidence still does not solve the problem of Lucian in the Pentateuch".

[8] Cf. N. Fernández Marcos, "The Lucianic Text in the Books of Kingdoms". In *De Septuaginta. Studies in honour of John William Wevers*, 161-174, p. 168.

[9] Cf. E. Ulrich, *The Qumran Text of Samuel and Josephus*, Missoula Mont. 1978 and E. Tov "Lucian and Protolucian. Toward a new solution of the Problem". *RB* 79 (1972) 101-113.

[10] N. Fernández Marcos, "La edición de las 'Quaestiones in Reges et Paralipomena' de Teodoreto". *Sefarad* 40, 2 (1980) 235-253 and N. Fernández Marcos-J.R. Busto Saiz, *Theodoreti Cyrensis Quaestiones in Reges et Paralipomena*, Madrid 1984, p. XLIV-LXIV.

Chronicles. Thus, for the first time we have tried to produce a critical edition of the Antiochene text, rescuing it from the scattered state
of fragmentation to be found in the apparatus of Brooke-McLean.
We hope that Lagarde's provisional work has now been corrected.
We offer the Septuagint text such as it was read in the area of
Antioch in the 4th-5th century A.D. For this purpose we have col-
lated anew the five Lucianic manuscripts for 1-2 Samuel (seven for
1-2 Kings), using Theodoret's text critically restored as a singular
witness for establishing the Antiochene text. In a second apparatus
of witnesses the indirect evidence is presented in support of the
Antiochene text; first of all the Qumran testimony, then Josephus
colated anew by M.V. Spottorno, the rest of the Antiochene Fathers,
the evidence of the *Vetus Latina* and that of the Armenian version that
has been prepared by P. Cowe of Columbia University. I do not
need to emphasize the relevance of the new evidence coming not
only from the critical editions of the Fathers, but especially from the
study of the *Vetus Latina* and the Armenian version. As for the Latin,
we have had the opportunity of using Morano's edition of the Marginal Notes with *Vetus Latina* readings in Spanish Vulgata Bibles for
the books of Samuel and Moreno's edition of the same material for
the books of Kings. This is the first critical edition of a family of
manuscripts that transmit the main mass of the *Vetus Latina* readings
for Samuel-Kings only quoted until now according to a very faulty
copy edited by Vercellone[11]. For the Armenian version, Cowe's
collations are based on six manuscripts whose high quality had been
proved in Ruth's edition, where the secondary character of Zohrab's
edition (used by Brooke-McLean) has been shown[12].

The Antiochene text for Samuel-Kings stands out as a homogene-
ous text that has escaped the *kaige* revision. Nevertheless it is a revised and edited text with some recurrent and consistent features
rightly analysed by Brock[13]. They consist of a) stylistic improvements tending to avoid the semitisms of translation Greek, b) a frequent varying of synonyms that produces a high number of lexical

---

[11] C. Morano Rodríguez, *Glosas marginales de Vetus Latina en las Biblias Vulgatas
Españolas. 1-2 Samuel*, Madrid 1989 and A. Moreno Hernández, *Las glosas marginales
de* Vetus Latina *en las Biblias Vulgatas españolas*, Madrid 1992.

[12] N. Fernández Marcos-J.R. Busto Saiz, *El texto antiqueno de la Biblia Griega I.
1-2 Samuel*, Madrid 1989.

[13] S.P. Brock, *The Recensions of the Septuagint Version of 1 Samuel*, Ph.D. dissertation, Oxford University 1966, 229-305.

variants and c) a tendency, not consistently followed, to substitute
Attic forms for Hellenistic ones. Other corrections are best explained
as accommodations of the text for public reading[14].

Beside the linguistic features just mentioned one has to pay attention to a series of editorial and literary characteristics that contribute
to emphasize the strong peculiarity of this recension as a branch of
the Septuagint tradition. It cannot be forgotten that the Antiochene
text is first of all that of the Septuagint, as can be realised by a simple
comparison with the Hebrew text of Kings. The Antiochene text
shares with the rest of the Septuagint the additions of 1 Kings 2,35a-o
and 46a-l, concerning Salomon's wisdom and prosperity, both missing in the Hebrew. Likewise it shares with the rest of the Septuagint
tradition 1 Kings 12,24a-z, which has no equivalent in the Masoretic text (this is a section also omitted in the Hexaplaric recension and
in manuscripts under Hexaplaric influence)[15]. Only ms.c_2 omits
this section here and gives a new recension of 1 Kings 14,1-20, a
conflation of the Hexaplaric recension and of the Lucianic one as I
have tried to show in a recent article[16]. Moreover, the Antiochene
text coincides with the rest of the Septuagint against the Masoretic
text in the different order of the material from 1 Kings 4,17 to chapter 8, and from 10,23 to chapter 17, as well as in the permutation
of chapters 20 (Ahab's victory) and 21 (Jezebel and Nabot's vine-
yard), chapters now attested in the *Vetus Latina*, thanks to the new
material recovered from the Marginal Notes of the Spanish Vulgata
Bibles[17].

But this once said, the editorial and literary interventions in the
Antiochene text should be no less stressed: as is well known, these
are the continuation of 2 Samuel up to David's death (1 Kings 2,12);
the omission of Josaphat's history in 1 Kings 22,41-51 because according to the Septuagint chronology, it has been told in 1 Kings
16,28a-h; as well as several rearrangements of the material, espe-

[14] Brock, *The Recensions*, p. 261-263.

[15] N. Fernández Marcos, "Literary and Editorial Features of the Antiochian
Text in Kings". In *VI Congress of the International Organization for Septuagint and Cognate
Studies*, ed. C. Cox, Atlanta 1987, 287-304, p. 290.

[16] N. Fernández Marcos, "En torno al texto hexaplar de 1 Re 14,1-20". *Sefarad*
46, 1-2 (1986) 177-190.

[17] Cf. A. Moreno Hernández, "Glosas inéditas de *Vetus Latina* en manuscritos
españoles: aportaciones para la reconstrucción de 1 Re 20". *Sefarad* 48, 2 (1988)
343-356 and ——, "Nuevas glosas de *Vetus Latina* (1 Re. 22). Edición y estudio".
Emerita 58 (1990) 275-287.

cially in 2 Kings 9-17[18]. Editorial intervention seems clear also in the addition of 2 Kings 10,36-43, supported by the *Vetus Latina* and in the thorough rearrangement of chapter 13. Both have been differently interpreted by Rahlfs and Trebolle: for the former they are basically of secondary character, and for the latter they are more ancient than the majority text[19]. Interestingly enough the *Papyrus Vindobonensis* also exhibits a large number of changes in this section, probably connected with a former stage of the text transmission in its Greek model[20].

Editorial activity can also be detected in a series of procedures tending to the harmonization of the narrative. In Kings I have noticed the following corrective mechanisms peculiar to the Antiochene text: A) The completion of the "unsaid" in the prediction/fulfilment scheme, a technique used by a creative copyist, without equivalence in the Hebrew or in the majority text of the Septuagint. Even if we concede that this tendency started with the Septuagint translation of Kings, or with its *Vorlage*, or in 4QSam[a] (as compared with the Masoretic text) as Pisano claims[21], this tendency is much more developed at the stage reflected by the Antiochene text than in the majority text of the Septuagint. And this fact requires some explanation. B) The addition of small sentences, in order to clarify the narrative or to smooth some breaks in the meaning. It is noteworthy that such additions are not usually taken from parallel passages, nor can they be shown to be double translations from the Hebrew, but rather they are inner Greek editorial changes, more related to the technique of the redaction of a narrative[22]. This procedure is very common among medieval copyists of historiographi-

---

[18] N. Fernández Marcos, "On the Present State of Septuagint Research in Spain". In *La Septuaginta en la investigación contemporánea (V Congreso de la IOSCS)*, Madrid 1985, 271-285, p. 280-283.

[19] Cf. A. Rahlfs, *Septuaginta-Studien 3*, Göttingen 1911, p. 276-277. J. Trebolle, *Jehú y Joas*, Valencia 1984, p. 110-125.

[20] Cf. B. Fischer with the collaboration of E. Ulrich and Judith E. Sanderson, "Palimpsestus Vindobonensis: A Revised Edition of L 115 for Samuel-Kings". *BIOSCS* 16 (1983) 13-87, p. 26-27 and P.-M. Bogaert, in *RevBén* XCV (1985) p. 177: "Il serait téméraire de ne pas tenir compte de ce témoin dans la critique littéraire de IV R. X-XVII".

[21] S. Pisano, *Additions or Omissions in the Books of Samuel*, Freiburg/Göttingen 1984, p. 67 and 165. The edition of the unpublished material from Qumran would contribute enormously to illuminate the whole process and help to understand even the evolution of the Biblical text towards paraphrase, re-written Bible etc.

[22] J. Trebolle, *Centena in Libros Samuelis et Regum*, Madrid 1989, p. 23-25.

cal works[23]. C) The stylistic rewriting of the text, including a change to hyperbaton, the elimination of the semitisms typical of translation Greek, the change of synonyms and an addition of Atticising colouring, the restoration of the logical order of the sentence etc.[24]. This technique has its counterpart too in the transmission of some medieval works where the copyists recast the narrative according to diverse criteria of actualization. In this process the texts sometimes even take on the linguistic traits of the copyist, as is reflected in the stylistic corrections of the Antiochene recension[25].

Finally, leaving aside some midrashic or merely cultured corrections, the Antiochene text stands out by its numerous double readings extensively treated by Rahlfs[26]. Double readings constitute a part of Septuagint research that deserves a deeper and more systematic treatment[27]. The origin of the double readings is very varied. They can emerge at the level of the translation technique or be a product of the text transmission. The copyist or editor tries to create a new meaning by including in different sentences those words that originally represented either alternative translations for a difficult original passage, or simply synonymous readings intended to reflect the diverse shades of meaning of the Hebrew original. The word in question is rendered twice, or it is transliterated and translated, while the rest of the sentence is rendered once[28].

The Antiochene recension excels in this technique, as Driver pointed out[29]. No doubt, some of these readings come from parallel passages that tend to complete or elucidate the narrative. But we cannot overlook a good number of double readings that are rooted in the Hebrew, either as conflations of the translation plus transliter-

---

[23] A. Blecua, *Manual de crítica textual*, Madrid 1983, p. 161-163.

[24] Examples in Fernández Marcos, "Literary and Editorial Features", p. 295-296.

[25] Blecua, *Manual de crítica textual*, p. 164: "Este es el caso de la versión leonesa y castellana de Alexandre, los riojanismos de Berceo, los aragonesismos de las *Vitae Patrum* de Gonzalo de Santa María".

[26] Rahlfs, *Septuaginta-Studien*, p. 192-199.

[27] Cf. Z. Talshir, "Double Translations in the Septuagint". In *VI Congress of the IOSCS*, p. 21-63.

[28] On the different possibilities of double readings cf. Talshir, "Double Translations", p. 33-36.

[29] Cf. S.R. Driver, *Notes on the Hebrew Text and the Topography of the Books of Samuel*, Oxford 1913, 2nd. edition, LVII: "When Lucian found in MSS two divergent readings of a passage, he systematically combined them, producing thereby what could be called in the terminology of the NT criticism 'conflate' readings".

ation of the same Hebrew word, or as alternative readings based on a different vocalization of the Hebrew, or as alternative readings based on a different consonantal text. There are plenty of examples that could be adduced[30]. It must be stressed that many of these originated in an alternative reading of the Masoretic text without connection with the Hexapla, and that in all probability these readings represent an early layer of the tradition, closer to the level of translation technique than to the level of text transmission[31]. Moreover, the Antiochene text has been shown to be rooted in a Hebrew text often different from the Masoretic text. So far it can be said in those cases in which the Antiochene readings are in disagreement with the Masoretic text and they are supported by the Hebrew tradition stretching from the Qumran evidence to the Medieval Hebrew manuscripts. First of all in the *kaige* sections of Samuel, 4QSam[a] agrees in a higher proportion with the Antiochene recension than with the majority text of the Septuagint[32]. Secondly, when we dispose of abundant material (as in the parallel passages of 2 Sam 22 and Psalm 18; 2 Kings 18-20 and Isaiah 36-39) it has been shown that the Old Latin of Kings, which faithfully reflects the Antiochene text, is very close to the stage of text represented by the Masoretic text of Isaiah[33]. Thirdly, when we take into account the striking

---

[30] Cf. Fernández Marcos, "Literary and Editorial Features of the Antiochian Text in Kings", p. 297-298.

[31] As Talshir points out, "The abundance of double translations rather indicates that he (i.e. the translator or redactor) must have been using other translations in the process of creating his own work", cf. Talshir, "Double Translations", p. 46. See also I.L. Seeligmann, "Indications of editorial alteration and adaptation in the MT and the Septuagint". *VT* 11 (1961) 201-221, p. 202: "There is no doubt that in these stages which, in a sense, constitute the prehistory of the Massorah, the copyists did not confine themselves to the preservation of what was already there but both corrected and invented"; and on p. 215 concernimg the Septuagint he continues: "On occasion transliterations of Hebrew words into Greek letters were incomprehensible, and were fashioned into, as it were, Greek words. Such transformations as well as other corruptions in the Greek text often required continuation and expansion in order to harmonize the corrupt version with the requirements of grammar and relevancy. In addition we find that scribes may interpret an incoherent text 'midrashically', adding things which at times do not at all accord with the intentions of the original author". Cf. S. Talmon, "Conflate Readings (OT)". In *IDBS*, p. 170-173.

[32] Cf. E. Ulrich, *The Qumran Text of Samuel and Josephus*, p. 257-261.

[33] Cf. A. Catastini, *Isaia ed Ezechia*, p. 265-266. In 2 Samuel 22 Busto Saiz has realized that some of the Antiochene readings are supported by the Masoretic Text of Psalm 18, cf. J.R. Busto Saiz, "The Antiochene Text of 2 Samuel 22". In *VIII Congress of the International Organization for Septuagint and Cognate Studies*, Atlanta Georgia 1994 (in press).

agreements between the Antiochene variants and the Hebrew variants other than Masoretic. As Wevers concluded "the Hebrew variants are remnants of the Hebrew Vorlage used by the first translators of the O.T., as well as of Hebrew readings in vogue at the time of the later revisers"[34].

To sum up, we are dealing with an edited text that preserves sufficient traces of redactional activity and the colouring of the Greek of the time, reflected in multiple stylistic improvements as well as in slight Atticization. Nevertheless this text preserves many ancient readings and it has been proved that it is rooted in the Hebrew.

Should we rest content with this restoration of the Antiochene text, as read in the Antioch of the 4th-5th centuries, or is it possible to go a step further in the search for the Old Greek? I realize that with our edition the Old Greek of the Septuagint is far from restored. I fully subscribe to Wever's words concerning this topic: "Aber die Gleichsetzung des boc^2e^2 Textes mit der unrevidierten LXX ist m.E. nicht beweisbar...Alles was wir mit Sicherheit schliessen können ist dies: wenn der B-Text von Sam-Kön die Arbeit des R-Revisors im l. Jahrh. ist, dann gibt es für diesen Abschnitt keine unrevidierte LXX"[35]. Text criticism has its own, strict rules. Each reading must be examined according to these rules, taking into account the development of the Greek language and everything we know of the whole text transmission before labeling it as the Old Greek.

The critical restoration of the Old Greek cannot be mixed methodologically with the examination of the process of literary composition and growth of the book, nor with the question of the priority of the different texts. Statements claiming that many reconstructions of the original Hebrew of Kings must take into account the Antiochene text and the *Vetus Latina*[36] may be true from the literary point of view but they are hardly true from the perspective of text criticism. Because, in fact, we are crossing the frontier between text criticism and literary criticism. At the utmost, it can be proved which text tradition is to be preferred according to the literary patterns of composition; a question slightly different from the problem of the

---

[34] Wevers, "A Study in the Hebrew Variants in the Books of Kings", p. 75.

[35] Wevers, "Septuaginta-Forschungen seit 1954", p. 75.

[36] J. Trebolle, "From the 'Old Latin', through the 'Old Greek' to the 'Old Hebrew'". *Textus* XI (1984) 17-36.

original text. In other words, at this stage we are comparing not variant readings, but different redactions. In fact we are performing
literary criticism carried out by means of redactions preserved in
different languages[37].

Neither can the Old Greek be restored from heterogeneous elements. At times the *Vetus Latina* may be a better witness of the original but it cannot be restored or retroverted simply as the Old Greek,
because the *Vetus Latina* cannot be identified with the Old Greek nor
with the Antiochene text.

In all probability the Old Greek of Samuel-Kings-Chronicles will
not look very different from the Antiochene text now critically edited. In spite of that it cannot be identified with the Antiochene text
and it has to be reconstructed by a minute analysis and discussion
of each variant in the light of the whole Greek tradition duly stratified. In this perspective our edition is only one step forward in
the process of reconstruction of the Old Greek of Samuel-Kings-
Chronicles, but it is—I hope—a very important step.

---

[37] In my opinion there is a danger in our days not only of combining different
methods of low and high criticism, but of confusing them also even in terminology.
For the Biblical books as a whole most part of the links in the chain of text transmission are missing. Several times we can only speculate on some of the stages along
this process. Only in a few cases when we dispose of abundant material—as in the
parallel passages especially—can we catch a glimpse of the real text history.

ABERRANT TEXTS IN THE BOOKS OF KINGS

CHAPTER FOUR

NEW EVIDENCE FROM THE OLD LATIN: A PECULIAR TEXT

Last year I spoke on the Septuagint text history emphasizing the diversity of its texts and focusing on a concrete text, the Antiochene or Lucianic one in the Historical Books.

In this series of Lectures I will concentrate on the problems arising from the textual form of a secondary version, the Old Latin of those books, a version dependent on the Septuagint and closely related to the Antiochene text. I hope that the following reflections may shed some light on a question that fills the horizon of Biblical text criticism in the last two decades: the plurality of texts detected in the Historical books since the Qumran documents have been incorporated into the history of the Biblical text. The debate concerning the textual groups has only started, and theories like that of the "local texts" (F.M. Cross, putting the emphasis on geography), the diverse communities supporting those texts (S. Talmon, putting the emphasis on sociology and religion), or merely "a series of texts" (E. Tov), have been submitted recently to hard criticism in part due to the new evidence coming from the unedited Biblical texts of Qumran[1] and in part due to a lack of methodological accuracy. Biblical text criticism has forgotten, in the words of B. Chiesa, the main rules that caused this science to be respected in the realm of Classical Philology, the grouping of witnesses not by agreements and disagreements among them but by means of common errors. Let us remember the words of Housman: "Textual criticism is (...) the art of discovering error in texts and the art of removing it. That is its definition, that is what the name denotes"[2].

In this evocative year of 1992, in which Spain remember non only its encounter with the New World but also the publication of the first

---

[1] Cf. F. García Martínez, "Las fronteras de lo bíblico". *Scripta Theologica* 23, 3 (1991) 759-784.

[2] Cf. B. Chiesa, "Textual History and Textual Criticism of the Hebrew Old Testament". In *The Madrid Qumran Congress* I, p. 267 quoting the famous sentence of A.E. Housman, *The Application of Thought to Textual Criticism*, PCA 12 (1922) 67-84 = *The Classical Papers of A.E. Housman*, III, Cambridge 1972, p. 1058-1069.

grammar of the Spanish language by Elio Antonio de Nebrija ("que siempre la lengua fue compañera del Imperio" as he says in the Preface of his grammar devoted to the Catholic Queen Elisabeth), perhaps it is suitable to emphasize that the material I will deal with comes almost exclusively from Spain: a family of five Spanish Vulgate Bibles, mss 91-95 according to the classification of the *Vetus Latina Institut* in Beuron (Germany), that preserve in their marginal notes one of the most important repositories of Old Latin texts for Samuel-Kings. These manuscripts were copied between the Xth and XVIth century in the scriptoria of monasteries placed along the route of Saint James (Valvanera and San Millán de la Cogolla in La Rioja, Valeránica in Burgos and San Miguel de Escalada in León). The geographical position of Spain, on the extreme periphery of Europe, no doubt contributed to the preservation of such ancient texts in spite of the official policy then ruling to extend the Vulgate.

It is clear that Kahle relied on the older secondary translations made from the Greek Bible as some of the main witnesses for earlier texts of the Septuagint[3]. He was aware of the discrepancy in quotations by some of the Latin Fathers, such as Isidore of Sevilla[4], in relation to the Greek and Hebrew texts. He pays some attention to the Hebraisms of the Coptic versions too[5]. But, surprisingly enough, he does not treat systematically the numerous divergences of the *Vetus Latina* that could provide more support for his hypothesis about the plural or targumic origin of the Greek Bible.

Far from Kahle's theory as we may be, nevertheless it seems to me unevoidable today to include the *Vetus Latina* evidence in the present discussion on the textual pluralism or textual diversity of some of the Old Testament books. Let us consider, for instance, the divergent texts of *Vetus Latina* in books like Tobit or Esther, the striking additions without equivalence in Hebrew or Greek in some of the Wisdom books like Proverbs, Ben Sira or the Wisdom of Solomon, the strange rearrangement of the material in Jeremiah, Isaiah, Ezechiel or Daniel, the peculiar textual form of the Old Latin at the end of Joshua or in chapters 36-40 of Exodus etc.[6]. A typical case

---

[3] Cf. P. Kahle, *The Cairo Geniza*, Oxford 1959 (2nd. edition), p. 262-264.

[4] Cf. Isidore of Sevilla (VI-VII centuries), *De Fide Catholica contra Judaeos* in Migne, *PL* 83, 449-583.

[5] Kahle, *The Cairo Geniza*, p. 262-263 and p. 258-261.

[6] As a background is the problem, still unresolved, of the unity or plurality of

of the disagreements between the *Vetus Latina* and the Biblical texts known until now is to be found in the books of Kings too.

In the introduction to our edition of "El texto antioqueno de la Biblia Griega. I 1-2 Samuel" I made the following statement: "Perhaps it is with regard to the Vetus Latina where the present edition breaks most new ground in comparison with earlier editions, especially for the retrieval of new material"[7]. The same could be said of

---

the *Vetus Latina*. Cf. R. Hanhart, *Text und Textgeschichte des Buches Tobit*, Göttingen 1984, p. 16-18; ——, *Septuaginta. VIII/3, Esther*, Göttingen 1966, p. 17-26 and J.T. Milik, "Les modèles araméens du livre d'Esther dans la Grotte 4 de Qumrân". *RQ* 15 (1991) 321-409. M. Revilla, "La Biblia de Valvanera". *La Ciudad de Dios* 120 (1920) 190-210, p. 203-210 and J. Schildenberger, *Die altlateinische Texte des Proverbienbuches*. Texte und Arbeiten I, p. 32-33, Beuron 1941, 63-143. J. Ziegler, *Septuaginta. XII/1 Sapientia Salomonis*, Göttingen 1962, p. 22-25 and ——, "Zur griechischen Vorlage der Vetus Latina in der Sapientia Solomonis". *Lex tua veritas. Festschrift Hubert Junker*, Trier 1961, p. 275-291; ——, *Septuaginta. XII/2 Sapientia Iesu Filii Sirach*, Göttingen 1965, p. 23-29: VL is the only witness that can guide us in the reconstruction of the original order in Sir 30, 25-33, 16a and 33, 16b-36, 10; W. Thiele, *Vetus Latina. 11/2 Sirach (Ecclesiasticus), Freiburg 1988*, p. 110-112 and —— 24. *Bericht des Vetus Latina Institut*, Beuron 1991, p. 31-32; G. Haendler, "Zur Arbeit an altlateinischen Bibelübersetzungen". *TLZ* 114/1 (1989) 1-11, p. 9 points out on the Old Latin text of Ben Sira: "Viele Verse des lateinischen Textes haben in der erhaltenen griechischen Tradition keine Entsprechung, manche sind Doppelübersetzungen, stehen aber im Lateinischen dann in einem anderen Zusammenhang". P.-M. Bogaert, "Le Centre de recherche sur la Bible latine", p. 4; ——, "Le témoignage de la Vetus Latina dans l'étude de la tradition des Septante. Ezéchiel et Daniel dans le papyrus 967". *Bib* 59 (1978) 384-395. J.-C. Haelewyck, "Le cantique de la vigne. Histoire du texte vieux latin d'Is 5,1-7 (9a)". *ETL* 65 (1989) 257-279. T. Ayuso Marazuela, "Los elementos extrabíblicos del Octateuco". *EB* 4 (1945) 35-60, p. 54-58 y —— *La Vetus Latina Hispana. II El Octateuco*, Madrid 1967, p. 276-277. *La Bible d'Alexandrie. 2 L'Exode* par Alain Le Boulluec et Pierre Sandevoir Paris 1989, p. 66. Cf. A. Dold, "Versuchte neu—und erstergänzungen zu den altlateinischen Texten im Cod. Clm 6225 der Bayer. Staatsbibliothek". *Bib* 37 (1956) 39-58.
Concerning the possible diverse *Vetus Latina* translations of the same biblical book Brock insists: "Obwohl dies in einigen Büchern der Fall gewesen sein mag, ist es viel wahrscheinlicher dass die altlateinischen Übersetzungen einem fortwährenden Prozess der Revision auf der Grundlage verschiedener griechischer Texte unterworfen waren. Als Folge davon enthält die Vetus Latina Material sehr unterschiedlicher Herkunft und sehr unterschiedlichen Wertes. Sie trägt möglicherweise Spuren einer hebraisierenden *correctio* in sich die in der erhaltenen griechischen Handschriftentradition keine Spuren hinterlassen hat. In den meisten Büchern können eine afrikanische und verschiedene europäische Texttypen herausgeschält werden", cf. S.P. Brock, "Bibelübersetzungen" in *Theologische Realenzyklopädie*, Band 6, Berlin-New York 1980, p. 177.

[7] "Tal vez sea esta área de la Vetus Latina donde nuestra edición presenta mas novedades frente a las ediciones anteriores sobre todo en lo que respecta a la recuperación de nuevos materiales", cf. N. Fernández Marcos—J.R. Busto Saiz, *El texto antioqueno de la Biblia Griega. I,1-2 Samuel*, Madrid 1989, p. XLV.

our edition of the Antiochene text for 1-2 Kings[8] recently appeared. We relied indeed on three recent critical editions, unknown to Brooke-McLean that present more than the 90% of the *Vetus Latina* material known until now for Samuel-Kings: 1) Diercks' edition of Lucifer of Cagliari that improves substantially on Hartel's edition of 1886[9]; 2) Fischer's new edition of the *Palimpsestus Vindobonensis,* that changes notably the textual image obtained from the Belsheim publication (Christiania 1885)[10]; and finally, 3) C. Morano's edition for 1-2 Samuel and A. Moreno's edition for 1-2 Kings of the Marginal Glosses of *Vetus Latina* in the Spanish Vulgate Bibles. As is well known, for his edition of the marginal notes in Samuel-Kings over a century ago Vercellone used a very faulty copy of the *Codex Gothicus Legionensis*—the *Vaticanus lat. 4859*[11]—Consequently the new editions have rescued a good deal of readings missing in Vercellone's publication[12]. Moreover, for 1-2 Kings A. Moreno has recovered 85 new glosses, 20 of them all over those books, but 65 belonging to seven specific chapters and concentrated especially on chapters 20-22 of 1 Kings. Those chapters are missing in Vercellone's edition because two folia of the copy used for his collations were lacking; this lacuna could be restored by Moreno through the collation of the whole family of Spanish manuscripts 92-94-95[13].

---

[8] N. Fernández Marcos-J.R. Busto Saiz, *El texto antioqueno de la Biblia griega. II 1-2 Reyes*, Madrid 1992, p. IX.

[9] G.F. Diercks, *Luciferi Calaritani Opera quae supersunt. CCSL VIII*, Turnholti/ Brepols 1978.

[10] B. Fischer with the collaboration of Eugene Ulrich and Judith E. Sanderson, "Palimpsestus Vindobonensis: A Revised Edition of L115 for Samuel-Kings". *BIOSCS* 16 (1983) 13-87.

[11] C. Vercellone, *Variae Lectiones Vulgatae latinae Bibliorum editionis*, II Roma 1964, pp. XCIII-XCIV.

[12] Cf. C. Morano Rodríguez, *Glosas marginales de Vetus Latina en las Biblias Vulgatas españolas. 1-2 Samuel*, Madrid 1989, p. XXXVIII-L, where we can appreciate that whole sentences were omitted by Vercellone in 1 Sam 4,1; 8,7; 11,10; 15,12; 17,40.43; 22,8; 23,3; 24,16; 25,32 and 2 Sam 1,6.9.10; 3,26; 9,7; 14,14; 18,2.3.6.11.29. A. Moreno Hernández, *Las glosas marginales de Vetus Latina en las Biblias Vulgatas españolas. 1-2 Reyes*, Madrid 1992, p. 75. According to the linguistic phenomena reflected in the Latin of the glosses these proceed from a version made between the late 2nd and the late 3rd century A.D. Their text was transformed into glosses to a Vulgate Bible *ca.* VIII-IX Century A.D. And the manuscripts that preserve the glosses come from a date between the Xth and the XVIth Century, Cf. Moreno Hernández, *Las glosas marginales*, p. 407-420.

[13] Cf. A. Moreno Hernández, "Glosas inéditas de 'Vetus Latina' en manuscritos españoles: Aportaciones para la reconstrucción de 1 Re 20". *Sefarad* 48, 2 (1988)

On the other hand and despite these contributions to the recovery of Vetus Latina texts for Samuel-Kings, it is still true that studies and bibliography on the Old Latin versions are very scarce in the field of the Old Testament. Modern commentaries and text critical studies pay little or null attention to the Old Latin[14]. Some years ago E. Ulrich made a tentative study of the *Vetus Latina* compared with the Hebrew fragments of Qumran[15]. In his accurate contribution, "Characteristics and Limitations of the Old Latin Translation of the Septuagint"[16], published five years later, Ulrich deals with a series of features of this translation drawn from the books of Samuel. But he does not mention those phenomena of the Old Latin version that resist interpretation or at least are not satisfactorily explained in terms of the translator's technique.

I shall not be dealing now with the general problems concerning the origin of the *Vetus Latina*, whether there were many or a unique translation, the question of its *Vorlage* and the problem of its contacts with the Hebrew text or tradition; all of these are disputable points on which agreement among scholars has not yet been reached and probably never will be[17]. I prefer to proceed rather by induction going from the evidence we have for a concrete book towards tentative conclusions within the limits of such a book.

In dealing with the *Vetus Latina* as a witness for the Antiochene text in the books of Samuel-Kings I found a considerable proportion of material with no support in the known manuscripts for those books. This material, with no equivalent in the known Biblical texts—whether Hebrew, Greek or Latin—required an explanation, because this phenomenon is strange, to say the least, in the transmission of a Biblical text. Certainly we find some expansions of the text

---

343-356, p. 345 and ——, "Nuevas glosas de 'Vetus Latina' (1 Re 22). Edición y estudio". *Emerita* 58 (1990) 275-287.

[14] D. Barthélemy, *Critique textuelle de l'Ancien Testament I*, Fribourg—Göttingen 1982; John Gray, *I and II Kings. A Commentary*, London 1974²; P. Kyle McCarter, *I Samuel*, New York 1980, *II Samuel*, New York 1984; M. Cogan and H. Tadmor, *II Kings*, New York 1988.

[15] E. Ulrich, "The Old Latin Translation of the LXX and the Hebrew Scrolls from Qumran". In *The Hebrew and Greek Texts of Samuel*, ed. E. Tov, Jerusalem 1980, p. 121-166.

[16] Appeared in *La Septuaginta en la investigación contemporánea*, ed. N. Fernández Marcos, Madrid 1985, p. 67-80.

[17] Cf. B. Kedar, "The Latin Translations". In *Mikra*, ed. M.J. Mulder, Van Gorcum 1988, 293-339, p. 300-310.

in the Targum, but not in the Hebrew or secondary versions known until now. Even these targumic additions are quite different from those found in the Old Latin; they are bound to the specific targumic technique, consisting of explanation, actualization and paraenetic exhortation, and they are concentrated on concrete passages, giving exegetical answers to theological difficulties[18]. Moreover, the peculiar text and expansions of the Old Latin does not coincide with the expansions found in the Targum.

The unique readings of Ms 9a1 in the Peshitta tradition are of a different kind too, because though unique compared with the rest of the Syriac witnesses they consist of agreements of this manuscript with the Masoretic Text[19]. Perhaps the closest parallel is to be found in some Qumran unedited texts called Biblical Paraphrases containing several para-Biblical additions, some identical with the Samaritan Pentateuchal additions, others unattested elsewhere[20]. In any case this phenomenon is extremely surprising, coming as it does from a version like the Old Latin traditionally considered very literal. Are they to be explained in connection with the translation technique being used? Did they emerge by accident as a product of a long and complex history of its transmission?, or should they be connected with a different *Vorlage*?

---

[18] R. Le Déaut, "Un phénomène spontané de l'herméneutique juive ancienne: le targumisme". *Bib* 52 (1971) 505-525; —— *Targum du Pentateuque I, Genèse*, Paris 1978, 43-62; ——, "The Targumim" in *The Cambridge History of Judaism. Volume Two: The Hellenistic Age*, edited by W.D. Davies and Louis Finkelstein, Cambridge 1989, 563-590, p. 588: "A supposedly literal text such as Onkelos does not hesitate to resort to frequent borrowings of parallel passages to complete a too laconic text". And *The Aramaic Bible. Volume 10: Targum Jonathan of the Former Prophets* by D.J. Harrington and A.J. Saldarini, Edinburgh 1987, 3-13. See also A. Sperber, *The Bible in Aramaic, Vol IVb. The Targum and the Hebrew Bible*, Leiden 1973, p. 198-210: Additions and p. 37-132 for the typology of the targumic variants, and A. Shinan, "Targumic Additions in Targum Pseudo-Jonathan". *Textus* XVI (1991) 139-155, p. 154: "The targumic tradition exhibits a solid and common custom as to the number and location of verses that may be expanded in these ways".

[19] Cf. M.P. Weitzman, "The Originality of Unique Readings in Peshitta Ms 9a1" in *The Peshitta: Its Early Text and History*, edited by P.B. Dirksen and M.J. Mulder, Leiden 1988, p. 225-258; M.D. Koster, "Which Came First: The Chicken or the Egg? The Development of the Peshitta of Genesis and Exodus in the Light of Recent Studies", *ibid.* p. 99-127 and P.B. Dirksen, "Some Remarks in Connection with the Peshitta of Kings". *OS* XXV (1989) 22-29.

[20] Cf. E. Tov, "The Textual Status of 4Q364-367 (4QPP)", In *The Madrid Qumran Congress* I, p. 43-83.

Concretely for 1-2 Samuel the *Vetus Latina* text transmitted by the mss 91-95 agrees with the Antiochene text for 50% in non-*kaige* sections and for 70% in the *kaige*-sections, while it agrees with the rest of the Septuagint (LXX rell.) for 13% in non-*kaige* sections and for 11% in the *kaige*-sections. At the same time I noticed that it remained for a good deal in disagreement with the Antiochene as well as with the LXX rell.: for 36% in non-*kaige* sections and for 18% in the *kaige*-sections. In other words, in the *kaige*-sections the proportion of agreements between the *Vetus Latina* and the Antiochene is relatively high, while the agreements with LXX rell. descend although not too much[21].

Lucifer has a higher proportion of singular readings (35%) compared with a slight preference for the Antiochene text (37%) and a considerable proportion of readings in accordance with LXX rell. (27%). Nevertheless it must be noted first, that these figures are only indicative, while characteristic readings of Antiochene are undoubtedly shared by Lucifer[22]; second, the high proportion of singular readings can be best explained in the frame of the Biblical quotations and as adaptations to the context.

Finally, the *Palimpsestus Vindobonensis* shares 32% of its readings in the non-*kaige* sections and 57% in the *kaige*-sections with the Antiochene, while a good deal of its readings follow the LXX rell. (41% in the non-*kaige* sections and 25% in the *kaige*-sections), and it disagrees with the Antiochene as well as with the LXX rell. in a lower proportion of readings (25% in the non-*kaige* sections and 17% in the *kaige*-sections)[23].

If we turn to 1-2 Kings we find the following figures: the text of the *Vetus Latina* transmitted by the mss 91-95 agrees with the Antiochene for 45% in the non-*kaige* sections and for 58% in the *kaige*-sections. It coincides with LXX rell. for 11% in the non-*kaige* sections and for 7% in the *kaige*-sections, while it disagrees with the Antiochene and the LXX-rell. for 43% in the non-*kaige* sections and for 34% in the *kaige*-sections[24].

Lucifer agrees with the Antiochene for 43%, with the LXX rell.

---

[21] Cf. N. Fernández Marcos-J.R. Busto Saiz, *El texto antioqueno de la Biblia griega. I, 1-2 Samuel*, Madrid 1989, p. XLVIII.

[22] Fernández Marcos-Busto Saiz, *El texto antioqueno*, p. LXII-LXIII.

[23] Fernández Marcos-Busto Saiz, *El texto antioqueno*, p. LI.

[24] N. Fernández Marcos-J.R. Busto Saiz, *El texto antioqueno de la Biblia griega. II, 1-2 Reyes*, Madrid 1992, p. XLIII.

for 21%, while he desagrees with the Antiochene as well as with the LXX rell. for 34%[25]. In the case of Lucifer we have not analysed the *kaige-* and non-*kaige* sections separately, because for 1 Kings we count with double the number of quotations that we have for 2 Kings. The same observation is valid for the books of Samuel, because all the quotations except one belong to 1 Samuel.

Palimpsestus Vindobonensis agrees with the Antiochene for 41% in the non-*kaige* sections and for 56% in the *kaige*-sections. It coincides with LXX rell. for 38% in the non-*kaige* sections and for 21% in the *kaige*-sections, while it disagrees with the Antiochene and the LXX rell. for 19% in the non-*kaige* sections and for 21% in the *kaige*-sections[26].

The textual picture to be obtained from the *Vetus Latina* in Samuel-Kings is not uniform, but from both the above mentioned figures and also from the qualitative analysis of the variants in question it can be concluded that the Greek text used as Vorlage for the translation had many characteristic features in common with the Antiochene, especially in the *kaige*-sections just because there it is the only Septuagint text that has not been revised[27]. Precisely that is the reason why in these sections the agreements of Antiochene with 4QSam[a-c] increase too[28]. No doubt several readings of the *Vetus Latina* follow the text tradition of the majority Septuagint in contrast with the Antiochene, or reproduce variants attested only by isolated Greek manuscripts[29].

As a matter of fact among the *Vetus Latina* material that disagrees with both the Antiochene and the LXX rell. there are some readings that agree with the Hebrew, as might have been expected either because of the influence of Hexaplaric material (not always preserved in the known witnesses) or because of contamination with the Vulgate tradition.

---

[25] Fernández Marcos-Busto Saiz, *El texto antioqueno. II*, p. LI.

[26] Fernández Marcos-Busto Saiz, *El texto antioqueno. II*, p. XLVII.

[27] For a minute analysis of these features cf. A. Moreno Hernández, *Las glosas marginales de Vetus Latina en las Biblias Vulgatas españolas. 1-2 Kings*, Madrid 1992, p. 163-189 where he arrives at similar conclusions.

[28] Cf. E. Tov, "The Textual Affiliations of 4QSam[a]". *JSOT* 14 (1979) p. 43.

[29] For this last case see 1 Sam 10,2: *In monte Beniamin et in Selom, in Bacallat salientes magnas fossas, et dicent tibi: Inventae sunt asinae, quas iisti quarere*, compared with the apparatus of Brooke-McLean *ad locum*; or 1 Sam 18,3: *Et disposuit Ionatha ad David testamentum in dilectione illius et animae ipsius.*

But I want to focus now on the number of readings (and sometimes full sentences) present in the *Vetus Latina* for Samuel-Kings and missing not only in the Septuagint and Vulgate traditions but also in the Hebrew text tradition. This amounts to over 30% of the material coming from the marginal glosses in the Spanish family of Vulgate manuscripts. The problem is not new and it has striking parallels in other books of the Old Testament too, but in my opinion it has not yet found a satisfactory explanation[30]. When did this material emerge? At the time of the translation itself, as a consequence of a particular targum-like translation technique or during the process of text transmission? Do those additions go back to a different Greek *Vorlage* no longer extant today? Are they in fact actual additions or mere doublets or triplets, the result of a cumulative process of amalgamation that brought in alternative readings and rearranged the narrative in a new context searching for a new meaning? Can the text history of the *Vetus Latina* itself shed some light on this problem, a translation never considered official and consequently never held as canonical and untouchable?[31]. Let us draw as a sample a typical item from the narrative of David and Goliath:

---

[30] For the *Vetus Latina* interpolations in the book of Proverbs in a family of Spanish Vulgata manuscripts cf. M. Revilla, *Fragmenta Biblica Scurialensia*, El Escorial 1920, p. 28-38 = *La Ciudad de Dios* 120 (1920) 203-210 and T. Ayuso Marazuela, "Los elementos extrabíblicos de los Sapienciales". *EB* 6 (1947) 187-223, p. 223 where he promises to devote a particular study to the interpolations to Proverbs, study that never appeared. On other extrabiblical elements in some Spanish Vulgata manuscripts coming from the *Vetus Latina* material see a series of articles by Ayuso Marazuela published in *Estudios Bíblicos* and elsewhere from 1943 to 1948. Cf. T. Ayuso Marazuela, "La Biblia de Lérida". *Universidad* 21 (1944) 25-68, p. 26-30; ——, "Los elementos extrabíblicos del Octateuco". *EB* 4 (1945) 35-60, p. 60; ——, "Los elementos extrabíblicos de la Vulgata". *EB* 2 (1943) 133-187; —— "Los elementos extrabíblicos de los Libros de los Reyes". *EB* 4 (1945) 259-296; —— "Los elementos extrabíblicos de los Paralipómenos, Esdras, Tobías, Judith y Esther". *EB* 5 (1946) 5-41; ——, "Los elementos extrabíblicos de Job y del Salterio". *EB* 5 (1946) 429-459.

[31] Cf. A.V. Billen, *The Old Latin Texts of the Heptateuch*, Cambridge 1927, p. 184: "The Latin text was perhaps at no period regarded as being in itself unalterable or authoritative in the sense that the LXX was; hence changes were made continuously and repeatedly, and hence in spite of an underlying unity the forms varied so much in later times that it seemed no great exageration to say that the forms of the Latin Version were as numerous as the MSS of it". Let us remember Augustine, *De Doctrina Christiana* 2,11: "...cuique primis fidei temporibus in manus venit codex Graecus...ausus est interpretari", and Jerome in his Preface to Joshua: "...maxime cum apud Latinos tot sint exemplaria quot codices, et unusquisque pro arbitrio suo vel addiderit vel subtraxerit quod ei visum est, et utique non possit verum esse quod dissonet".

1 Sam 17,49: Misit manum in sacciperio, et substulit inde lapidem unam, et misit in fundibalo *circumducens in giro manum suam, invocavit nomen Domini: Domine, dimitte nuntium tuum, qui praecedat lapidem fundibali huius*; et percussit alienigenam in fronte eius, et pertransiit lapis cassidem eius et cecidit in faciem suam.

Ant: καὶ ἐσφενδόνησε καὶ ἐπάταξε τὸν ἀλλόφυλον

MT: ויקלע ויך את הפלשתי

V: Et funda iecit et percussit Philisteum

We find no traces of the *Vetus Latina* addition, printed in italics, in the Greek nor in the Hebrew, the Vulgate, the Targum or the Syriac[32]. It looks like one of the targumic expansions, but there is no sign of this exegetical commentary in the Targum Jonathan to the Former Prophets[33]. Probably the addition is rooted in a Hebrew tradition but I have not found any trace of it in Josephus' *Antiquities*, nor in the re-writing of the narrative *Liber Antiquitatum Biblicarum* of Pseudo-Philo, nor in Ginzberg's *Legends of the Jews*[34]. Where does this addition come from? For lack of a better explanation I think we are dealing with a midrashic development of the statement in v. 47 that this fight is the Lord's fight (*quoniam Domini est haec pugna*). There is no evidence that suggests the possibility of a different *Vorlage*. But the presence of such an expansion in a version held to be very literal should at least make us reflect more deeply on the translation technique used for the Old Latin and on the borderline between biblical and parabiblical texts.

In brief, this new material of the marginal notes with no support on the known manuscripts—as said above 30%—is worth being analysed. Let us emphasize again the contrast between the use made of

---

[32] Cf. Rahlfs' commentary in the apparat of his manual edition to 1 Sam 17,49: "Pro ἐσφενδόνησεν fabulatur codex quidam latinae versionis antiquae: "misit in fundibulum...etc." according to Vercellone's edition, cf. A. Rahlfs, *Septuaginta, id est Vetus Testamentum Graece iuxta LXX interpretes*, Stuttgart 1935.

[33] Cf. A. Sperber, *The Bible in Aramaic II. The Former Prophets According to Targum Jonathan*, Leiden 1959 and E. Martínez Borobio, *Targúm Jonatán a los Profetas Primeros en tradición babilónica. Vol. II: I-II Samuel*, Madrid 1987.

[34] Josephus, *Ant. Jud. VI, 189-190*; D.J. Harrington, J. Cazeaux, C. Perrot and P.-M. Bogaert, *Pseudo-Philon, Les Antiquités Bibliques* (SC 229-230) Paris 1976, and L. Ginzberg, *The Legends of the Jews I-VII*, Philadelphia 1946. Certainly the text is not to be found in any of the witnesses mentioned but the tradition of the angel behind David and fighting for him can be traced in Pseudo-Philo's *Biblical Antiquities*, LXI, 8: "Et respiciens Allophilus vidit angelum et dixit: Non solus occidisti me, sed qui tecum aderat, cuius species non est sicut species hominis".

the Qumran documents—as fragmentary, unedited or hypothetical as they may be—in Biblical text criticism and the scanty attention paid to this considerable amount of *Vetus Latina* evidence in disagreement with the known Biblical texts.

Appendix

L$_{91\text{-}95}$	= Spanish Family of Vulgate Bibles
L$_{115}$	= *Palimpsestus Vindobonensis*
Lucifer	= Lucifer of Cagliari
Ant	= The Antiochene Text of the Septuagint
LXX rel	= The Majority Text of the Septuagint

Καίγε-*Sections in Samuel-Kings*

2 Samuel 10,1—1 Kings 2,11
1 Kings 22,1—2 Kings 25,30

	1-2 Samuel		1-2 Kings	Total
L$_{91\text{-}95}$				
No-καίγε sections				
= Ant	50%		45%	47,5%
= LXX rel	13%		11%	12%
≠ Ant/LXX rel	36%		43%	39,5%
Καίγε-sections				
= Ant	70%		58%	64%
= LXX rel	11%		7%	9%
≠ Ant/LXX rel	18%		34%	26%

	1-2 Samuel		1-2 Kings	Total
L$_{115}$				
No-καίγε sections				
= Ant	32%		41%	36,5%
= LXX rel	41%		38%	39,5%
≠ Ant/LXX rel	25%		19%	22%
Καίγε-sections				
= Ant	57%		56%	56,5%

= LXX rel	25%	21%	23%
≠ Ant/LXX rel	17%	21%	19%

Lucifer

= Ant	37%	43%	40%
= LXX rel	27%	21%	24%
≠ Ant/LXX rel	35%	34%	34,5% *

---

* These figures are only indicative. I do not claim for statistical accuracy since we are dealing with different kind of variants.

CHAPTER FIVE

TRANSLATION, CORRUPTION AND INTERPRETATION: THE GENESIS OF THE OLD LATIN VARIANTS

I shall try now, using the technique of textual criticism, to analyse the typology of the Old Latin singular readings, grouping them into different categories. In this way I hope at least to explain not only a good deal of the divergencies, but also to shed light on the underlying problem: are we dealing with a different text or with a corrupt text? Does the Old Latin text go back to a different *Vorlage* or is it the result of a peculiar translation technique? Can the *Vorlage* be recovered despite the changes made at the stage of the translation and despite the alterations made through the process of text transmission? Are we able to discern between phenomena due to translation's technique and those due to palaeographic corruption?

A. – The presence of double readings in the Old Latin and their explanation

The phenomenon of double readings is one of the most outstanding characteristics of the Old Latin. Following its tendency to incorporate into the text material coming from different sources—a tendency already present in the Antiochene text—the Old Latin exhibits an amalgam of double or conflated readings scattered throughout the narrative in new contexts and therefore not always easy to discover.

a) The formation of double readings by the juxtaposition of translation plus transliteration:

1.—1 Sam 13,18 (Saul's battle against the Philistines): *Et aliud agmen respiciens viam Gabee, quae tendit in convallem caprearum, in terra Saba, quae est desertum*[1]

---

[1] When not expressly indicated, all the examples adduced of the Old Latin are taken entirely from the marginal glosses edited by C. Morano Rodríguez, *Glosas*

Ant: καὶ ἡ ἀρχὴ ἡ τρίτη ἐπιβλέπουσα ἐπὶ τὴν Γαβαὰ τὴν ἐκκύπτου-
σαν ἐπὶ Γαῖαν τὴν Σαβαίν [+ τὴν ἔρημον *dpt*, cf. Brooke-McLean]

MT: וְהָרֹאשׁ אֶחָד יִפְנֶה דֶּרֶךְ הַגְּבוּל הַנִּשְׁקָף עַל גֵּי הַצְּבֹעִים הַמִּדְבָּרָה

V: Tertius autem verterat se ad iter termini inminentis valli
Seboim contra desertum.

And still another would take the border road overlooking the Valley of Hyenas toward the wilderness.

As a matter of fact the most literal translation of the Hebrew is
represented here by the Vulgate. LXX and Ant read probably
gaboah as hill or a place-name for *gebul*. In fact it is hard to think that
a word as common as *gebul* was not understood by the translators.
In the following Hebrew sentence ʿ*al gey ha-zeboʿim* the second part
of the syntagma has been transliterated as Σαβαίν in the whole tradition of the Septuagint, and the first part has been transliterated as
Γαι, developed by the Antiochene into Γαιαν(γααν c_2e_2) as a place-
name or attracted by the homophonic translation of *ge* (valley) by
γαιαν = earth[2]. Nevertheless the Hexaplaric tradition, concretely
Theodotion, rightly translates the Hebrew expression by τὴν κοιλάδα τῶν δορκάδων (the valley of the gazelles).

If we turn now to the narrative of the *Vetus Latina* we realize that
it has incorporated the Hebrew expression ʿ*al gey ha-zeboʿim* twice
into the text, that is, "in terra Saba" corresponding to the Ant
Γαῖαν τὴν Σαβαίν and "in convallem caprearum" corresponding to
Theodotion's translation τὴν κοιλάδα τῶν δορκάδων (αʹ τὴν φάραγ-
γα τῶν ὑαίνων).

Hypothetically we can present the genesis of the *Vetus Latina* text
in following stages: a) "Et aliud agmen respiciens Gabee quae tendit

---

marginales de Vetus Latina en las Biblias Vulgatas españolas. 1-2 Samuel, Madrid 1989 and
A. Moreno Hernández, *Las glosas marginales de Vetus Latina en las Biblias Vulgatas
españolas. 1-2 Reyes*, Madrid 1992. The Antiochene text is quoted according to
N. Fernández Marcos-J.R. Busto Saiz, *El texto antioqueno de la Biblia griega. I, 1-2
Samuel*, Madrid 1989; *II, 1-2 Reyes*, Madrid 1992. The Hebrew, according to *Biblia
Hebraica Stuttgartensia, 3rd. edition*, Stuttgart 1987. The Vulgate, according to R.
Weber, *Biblia Sacra iuxta Vulgatam versionem. I Genesis-Psalmi*, 2nd. edition, Stuttgart
1975. The Targum, when quoted, according to A. Sperber, *The Bible in Aramaic.
II The Former Prophets According to Targum Jonathan*, Leiden 1959.

[2] Cf. C. Fritsch, "Homophony in the Septuagint". *Proceedings of the Sixth World
Congress of Jewish Studies*, Jerusalem 1977, p. 115-120 and P. Walters edited by
D.W. Gooding, *The Text of the Septuagint. Its corruption and their Emendation*, Cam-
bridge 1973, p. 186-189. See also J. Barr, "Doubts about Homoeophony in the
Septuagint". *Textus* XII (1985) 1-77 with abundant bibliography on this subject.

in terram Saba" according to Antiochene; b) the finding (probably through contact with the Hexaplaric material) of the alternative reading τὴν κοιλάδα τῶν δορκάδων, a result of a better translation of the obscure Hebrew expression. Likewise the finding of the variant reading τὴν ἔρημον coming from a part of the Septuagint tradition (mss. dpt), and τὴν ὁδόν, a reading of LXX rel translated by "viam". And c) The amalgamation of these heterogeneous elements by a redactor, who intended to confer a meaning to the whole sentence by introducing nexuses of conjunction and subordination, as appears in the final redaction: "Et aliud agmen respiciens viam Gabee quae tendit in convallem caprearum, in terra Saba, quae est desertum"[3].

b) The conflation of different interpretations of the Hebrew Vorlage caused by the palaeographic confusion of similar letters, the transposition or permutation of consonants as well as by different vocalization.

It is possible that these entered the Vetus Latina *via* the Hexapla, but it cannot be excluded that their incorporation occurred at the level of translation, as alternative readings were found by the translators in the sources used by them.

2.—1 Sam 13,3: *Et Saul tuba cecinit in omnem terram dicens: Audiant Hebraei: Dereliquerunt servi*

The second part of this sentence has been transmitted by the Greek, the Masoretic Text and the Vulgate in the following form:

---

[3] There are several instances of this pattern in Kings. Another example of this phenomenon can be seen in 2 Kings 16,17, again a case of double readings produced by the amalgamation of translation plus transliteration: "Destruxit rex mascharath templi et mechonoth dissipavit subductis retinaculis cyrot, deduxit mare aereum quod a vitulis subterpositis sustinebatur". Cf. A. Moreno Hernández, *Las glosas marginales de Vetus Latina*, p. 199-204. The frequent transliterations from the Hebrew in the passage quoted, that are lacking in the Greek tradition or in the known Hexaplaric material, arise the hard question about the origin of such transliterations. This problem can only be solved throught a thorough study of all the transliterated material of the Old Latin. Fischer asserts that some double readings of the marginal glosses might come from VL manuscripts containing some kind of information on the Hexaplaric readings, cf. B. Fischer, *Vetus Latina. Die reste der altlateinischen Bibel. 2 Genesis*, Freiburg 1951, p. 21*. But it should be taken into account that the three younger translators, with the exception of Theodotion, rather translate than transliterate.

Ant and LXX rel: Ἠθετήκασιν οἱ δοῦλοι α᾽ ἀκουσάτωσαν οἱ
ἑβραῖοι
MT: ישמעו העברים
V: Audiant Hebraei.

Let the Hebrews hear, or better, The Hebrews have revolted, reading יפשעו or ימשעו on the basis of the Septuagint, because the first
translation makes no sense in this context.

In this case VL includes a double reading as part of the narrative.
It is worth noticing that this version is more expansionistic, so to
speak, than the Antiochene text in its tendency to incorporate all the
material found in the text tradition. ''Dereliquerunt servi'' corresponds to the interpretation of all the Greek tradition except Aquila; ''Audiant Hebraei'' reflects the literal translation of the Masoretic text. The double reading is attested only at the level of the VL,
but its origin and development can be followed through the Greek
translation, that read *dalet* instead of *res*, a common palaeographical
error in the Hebrew manuscripts[4] and probably also read יפשעו instead of ישמעו. These verbs share two letters in common and the
third is very similar in script. In addition, confusion between מ and
פ was frequent and confusion between שׁ and פ was possible, especially in script of the second century B.C. as can be proved by other
examples of similar confusions in the Septuagint translation[5].

Besides, ἀθετέω is the regular translation in the Septuagint for
פשע while this would be the only occasion of it having been used as
the translation of שמע. It is quite possible that the second translation
''audiant Hebraei'' was incorporated in the text of the *Vetus Latina*
from the Hexaplaric material, concretely from Aquila. But it cannot
be excluded that the amalgamation of this doublet is prehexaplaric,
because it betrays redactional activity concerned with meaning.
Other testimonies of *Vetus Latina*, including the *Palimpsestus Vindobonensis*, are missing for this passage.

---

[4] Cf. J. Weingreen, *Introduction to the Critical Study of the Text of the Hebrew Bible*,
Oxford 1982, p. 39-43. That is the cause of the frequent confusion between ארם
and אדם that has left traces in the Old Latin of 2 Kings 3,26 too.

[5] Cf. Weingreen, *Introduction*, p. 39 and P. Kyle McCarter, *I Samuel*, p. 290
(Textual note to 1 Samuel 17,53) and p. 369 (Textual note to 1 Samuel 23,1) where
the same word has led LXX into a double reading.

3.—2 Kings 9,24: *Et percussit Ioram. . . et decidens in terram mortuus est residens in genua sua*
  Ant and LXX rel: καὶ ἔκαμψεν ἐπὶ τὰ γόνατα αὐτοῦ
  MT: ויכרע ברכבו
  V: Statimque corruit in curru suo.
  And he collapsed in his chariot

The Greek translators probably read על ברכיו instead of ברכבו as given by the MT. Apart from the similarity of letters (with only one permutation)[6], this reading was favoured by the frequency of the syntagma "to bend the knee" in Biblical Hebrew as well as in the Septuagint. VL has lost contact with the original. Probably "decidens / residens" (to fall dawn / to contract or shrink) is a double translation of the Greek verb ἔκαμψεν. From this double reading, and having no contact with the Hebrew tradition (because all reference to the chariot is left out), the translator or redactor developed a double sentence by inserting "in terram mortuus est": this new sentence had indeed a meaning but one very different from the original meaning of the Hebrew and Vulgate. In any case it seems that this particular expansion is due to the creative activity of the translator or to the early transmission, having no contact with either the Hexapla or the Vulgate.

Interestingly enough, double readings due to palaeographic confusion can be detected at the level of the Hebrew, as in the above mentioned examples. But palaeografic corruption at the level of the Greek or Latin transmission can be also detected as a cause of diverse Old Latin readings. Let us look some samples of the latter:

4.—2 Kings 3,4: *Et Mosa rex Moab ferebat tributum regi Israel centum millia modium tritici, et centum hordei et lanas.*
  Ant: καὶ Μωσὰ βασιλεὺς Μωὰβ ἦν νωκήδ, καὶ ἦν φέρων φόρον καὶ ἐπιστρέφων τῷ βασιλεῖ Ἰσραὴλ ἑκατὸν χιλιάδας ἀρνῶν καὶ ἑκατὸν χιλιάδας κριῶν ἐπιπόκων.
  MT: ומישע מלך מואב היה נקד והשיב למלך ישראל מאה אלף כרים
ומאה אלף אילים צמר
  V: Porro Mesa rex Moab nutriebat pecora multa et solvebat regi

---

[6] Cf. Weingreen, *Introduction*, p. 43.

Israhel centum millia agnorum et centum millia arietum cum velleribus suis.

Now Mesha king of Moab was a sheep-breeder and he used to pay
tribute to the king of Israel: one hundred thousand lambs and the
wool of one hundred thousand rams[7].

The Hebrew tradition as well as the Greek and Latin of the Vulgate
present Mesha as a sheep-raiser. But the word נקד was hardly understood by the Greek translators. Here (as well as in Am 1,1:
νωκήδ, ἐν νακκαριμ, the other passage where it occurs in the Septuagint, a doublet of the Hebrew בנקדים) the word is presented in
transliteration. The Old Latin says nothing about Mesha being a
shepherd; even the transliteration of the Septuagint with its many
variants is omitted. Moreover it transforms the tribute of lambs and
rams into a new one of wheat and barley. The genesis of this curious
variant could be as follows: the Latin translator did not understand
the reference to Mesha as a shepherd, which is omitted; probably he
read or interpreted κριθῶν instead of κριῶν in his Greek text. Then
he probably substituted for ἀρνῶν/κριῶν the syntagma πυρῶν καὶ
κριθῶν that appears as a cliché since Homer. Consequently he re-
arranged the passage and left the last word lanas intact as the equivalent of the Greek word ἐπιπόκων[8].

5.—2 Sam 15,32: Cum venisset David usque ad Ros, et orasset ibi
Dominum, ecce ibi in obviam venit Chusi princeps amicorum David.

This case is relevant because VL follows the Lucianic manuscripts
even in their mistakes. "Princeps amicorum" is a literal translation
of ἀρχιέταιρος, the reading of the Lucianic mss. Only a comparison

---

[7] We find no traces of the peculiar Vetus Latina readings for this passage in the
quotations of the Fathers nor in any other Old Latin witness. Nevertheless the marginal glosses offer under the sigla Al. another literal translation: "Et Mosa rex
Moab erat pecuarius, et praestabat regi Israel ex subiectione centum millia agnos,
et centum millia arietes cum velleribus suis".
Most of the glosses are introduced by the sigla GR or IN GR, but some of them
are preceded by the sigla Al. All we can say of this last sigla is that it proceeds from
reinterpretations produced when the text of the Vetus Latina was transformed into
glosses, that is, at a time when it was no more possible a systemathic comparison
with the Greek originals. In other words, Al. cannot be identified with a concrete
source, cf. Moreno Hernández, Las glosas marginales de Vetus Latina en las Biblias
Vulgatas españolas, p. 214-224.
[8] Cf. Moreno Hernández, Las glosas marginales, p. 209.

with the original חושי הארכי allows us to restore Χουσεὶ ὁ 'Αρχί, ἑταῖρος Δαυίδ, Hushai the Archite, glossed in LXX, the *Vetus Latina* and Josephus as "David's friend"[9].

6.—1 Sam 25,22: *Usque ad canem mingentem.*
God do the same to me and more if I leave him a single mother's son alive by morning.

Antiochene and Vulgate translate literally the Hebrew עד הבקר משתין בקיר (ἕως πρωῒ οὐροῦντα πρὸς τοῖχον and "usque mane mingentem ad parietem" respectively), "anyone urinating against the wall", a synecdoche for 'male'. The Targum translates with another, less provocative, phrase "anyone knowing knowledge". Several Hebrew manuscripts introduce אור from verse 34 rightly translated by the *Vetus Latina* at this passage ("usque ad lucem mane"). Therefore, in all probability the reading of the VL here is the result of an inner corruption of the Latin transmission, a corruption that has succeeded because it fits well the radical meaning of the oath. Within the Old Latin transmission the corruption from 'mane' to 'canem', due to the two words sharing four letters in common, is the easiest hypothesis for this variant reading.

B. – The formation of double sentences from double readings in the Old Latin due to the translation or the transmission

This procedure can be best illustrated by means of the following examples:

7.—1 Sam 15,9: *Et omne opus pretiosum reservaverunt et omnia supervacua disperdiderunt.*
    Ant: πᾶν δὲ ἔργον ἠτιμωμένον καὶ ἀπεγνωσμένον, αὐτὸ ἐξωλόθρευσαν
MT: וכל המלאכה נמבזה ונמס אתה החרימו
    V: Quidquid vero vile fuit et reprobum hoc demoliti sunt.

---

9 Cf. Josephus, *Ant.* 7,203: συνήντησε δ' αὐτῷ φίλος ἀνὴρ καὶ βέβαιος Χουσὶς ὄνομα. "Princeps amicorum David", the same construction than "princeps vinifusorum" for ἀρχιοινοχοός and "princeps pistorum" for ἀρχισιτοποιός, cf. Genesis 40,2.

But all the property that was despised and rejected they did put under the ban (a translation based on the LXX in place of the unintelligible MT—nifal of בזה = 'despise' and of מסס = 'dissolve'—).

The text of the VL is also attested by Lucifer with the sole omission of "omnia". The first part of the sentence probably arose from the reading τιμωμένον accepted by the Latin translators instead of ἠτιμωμένον. The translation "pretiosum" needed to be completed with a verb like "reservaverunt" to give meaning within the new context. The second part corresponds very roughly to the Greek text. It should be noted that the Latin version introduces a stylistic device, namely *parallelismus membrorum*, lacking both in the original and in the rest of the versions[10]

8.—2 Sam 5,23: *In locum plaumonis prope cum coeperint plorare*
    Ant and LXX rel: πλησίον τοῦ κλαυθμῶνος
    MT: ממול בכאים
    V: Ex adverso pirorum.
    And approach them in front of Bachaim. Probably the name of a forest, a group of trees or plants (Vulgate understand "the pear trees").

The Old Latin translation derives from the etymological interpretation of the Septuagint itself that probably read הבכים or at least understand this in the light of the place-name *Bôkim*, that is, "weepers" according to the popular etymology of Judges 2,1-5 that connects this name with the root בכה = to weep[11]. Interestingly enough the Latin translator may have connected the Greek κλαυθμῶνος, place of weeping, with the Latin verb *plango* (which has the same meaning and a similar, homophonic sound) creating the neologism *plaumonis*, that is, half a loan-word and half a semantic copy

---

[10] Cf. J. Trebolle, "Reflejos de paralelismo hebreo en la Vetus Latina". *Sefarad* 46, 1-2 (1986) 463-471, p. 463: "El estudio de tales fenómenos de paralelismo en la VL permitiría reconocer en algún caso una estructura paralelística hebrea, con un texto diferente al representado por TM y LXX, y en otros casos una característica de traducción hebraizante de la 'Vetus Latina' o de una de sus formas textuales". See also L. Jiménez-Villarejo, "Estructuras poéticas en la Vetus Latina: Liber Sapientiae". *Actas del I Simposio de Latín Cristiano*, Salamanca 1990, p. 343-351.

[11] Cf. N. Fernández Marcos, "Nombres propios y etimologías populares en la Septuaginta". *Sefarad* 37 (1977) 239-259, p. 254.

(*calco*)[12]. The rest of the sentence "cum coeperint plorare" seems to be a development considered necessary for the full comprehension of the hapax legomenon *plaumonis*, as well as an explanation for a passage so much affected by a perplexing translation. In any case this expansion seems to be due to the inner development of the Old Latin tradition, be it at the level of the translation or at the level of the early transmission[13].

9.—1 Sam 3,13: *Quia contemnentes Deum male locuti sunt de Deo filii eius, et non monuit eos nec castigavit illos.*

Ant: ὅτι κακολογοῦντες θεὸν οἱ υἱοὶ αὐτοῦ, καὶ οὐκ ἐνουθέτει αὐτούς.

MT: כי מקללים להם בניו ולא כהה בם

V: Eo quod noverat indigne agere filios suos et non corripuit eos.

Because he (Eli) knew that his sons were blaspheming God and did not restrain them (*'elohim* was probably the original reading, altered in the Hebrew to *lahem* "to them")[14].

Given the Old Latin tendency to incorporate different translations into the narrative—a technique used more in this secondary version than in the Antiochene text—we can recognize in this passage traces of two double translations from the Greek: *contemnentes deum / male locuti sunt de deo* for κακολογοῦντες θεὸν, and *monuit / castigavit* for ἐνουθέτει. Moreover, the Greek version and the Old Latin support the original reading אלהים in the Hebrew altered by the scribes to להם in order to avoid that the name of God be connected with the word מקללים. Again the resulting sentence has a very different meaning from that of the source language.

10.—1 Kings 22,35: *Cum enim rex Israel staret in quadriga sua et ex diverso exercitus Syriae, in tantum profluxit sanguis vulneris eius ut sub pedibus quadrigae curreret flumen cruoris eius*[15]

---

12 Cf. Morano, *Glosas marginales*, p. LXXV.

13 For another explanation of this passage see P.-M. Bogaert in his review of Morano's book in *RevBén* 1990: "Bulletin de la Bible Latine", p. 291: the Latin translator took the word for a place-name and added a popular etymology as explanation.

14 Cf. McCarter, *I Samuel*, p. 96: "Deliberate scribal distorsion in MT for pious reasons, the passage being among those few recognized in Rabbinic sources as well as the Masoretic lists as belonging to the so-called *tiqqune sôpherim*, 'emendations of the scribes'".

15 This sentence belongs to the new material from the marginal glosses recovered for chapters 20-22 of 1 Kings. Claude of Turin seems to know it, since in

Ant: καὶ ὁ βασιλεὺς ἦν ἑστηκὼς ἐπὶ τοῦ ἅρματος ἐξ ἐναντίας Συρίας ἀπὸ πρωῒ ἕως ἑσπέρας, καὶ ἐξεπορεύετο τὸ αἷμα τῆς πληγῆς τῆς τροπώσεως καὶ ἀπέθανεν ἑσπέρας ὁ βασιλεύς, καὶ ἐξεπορεύετο τὸ αἷμα τῆς τροπῆς ἕως τοῦ κόλπου τοῦ ἅρματος.

MT: והמלך היה מעמד במרכבה נכח ארם וימת בערב ויצק דם המכה אל חיק הרכב

V: Et rex Israhel stabat in curru suo contra Syros et mortuus est vesperi, fluebat autem sanguis plagae in sinum currus.

And the king was propped up in his chariot facing the Aramaeans and he died at evening and the blood of his wound poured down into the body of his chariot.

The Antiochene text provides traces of redactional activity by placing the effusion of the blood before the death of the king, that is, by enumerating twice the action mentioned once in the Hebrew. But the Old Latin here is a model of literary remoulding of the Greek narrative. Struck by the cumbersome doublet of the Greek, it transforms the text into a new narrative that condenses the redaction of the Septuagint, introduces subordination for coordination, and at the same time succeeds in achieving a sentence full of sonority. Here the intense redactional activity of the translator is apparent: he changes juxtaposition into subordination (*cum enim...*, *in tantum ...ut*) in order to articulate the double reading of the Septuagint in a new sentence, completely remoulded from the point of view of syntax and, above all, of style. The death of the king, in the original put out of logical sequence, is suggested in the Old Latin but not expressly stated, as in the Greek and the Hebrew; the Old Latin also omits the time of the battle (בערב in the Masoretic Text, ἀπὸ πρωῒ ἕως ἑσπέρας in Antiochene). Other changes can easily be explained, for instance, the mention of the *exercitus*, absent from the other texts, probably arose from a corruption of ἐναντίας (= *diverso*) read as στρατιᾶς. Consequently I would consider it as a double reading of ἐναντίας.

Once again, the supposed literalism of the VL is more nuanced, allowing a certain initiative in the rearrangement of the material, not only for the sake of clearer meaning but to achieve a better stylistic construction. Usually when a passage is obscure or the translator

---

Rg.q. 31 he quotes: "sanguis enim, qui *defluxit* de corpore eius, et *cucurrit* in lectum currus, ex corio erat".

is faced by a perplexing translation, VL adopts a text twice as long in order to clarify the original. But sometimes VL also condenses and remoulds the material, creating a new meaning often far from that of the original[16].

C. – Midrashic expansions, exegetical interpretations and editorial notes that bear witness to an intense redactional activity by the translators or early copyists. Such expansions can be the result of
a) The perplexity of the translator over a difficult passage in the original:

11.—1 Sam 26,5: *Saul dormiebat in stragulis praeclaris*
Ant: καὶ Σαοὺλ ἐκάθευδεν ἐν λαμπήνῃ
MT: ושאול שכב במעגל
V: (cumque vidisset) Saulem dormientem in tentorio.
Now Saul was laying within the encampment, with the troops encamped all around him.

The Hebrew מעגל means (according to Koehler-Baumgartner) "circle of a camp"; "anillo del castro" in the Spanish translation of F. Cantera, "within the lines" according to the New English Bible[17]. The Septuangint as well as Antiochene translate by λαμπήνη, that is, "a chariot covered with canopy". The Vulgate follows the interpretation of Theodotion, σκήνη. The Old Latin in all probability introduces a perplexing translation trying to cope with a passage of difficult comprehension for the contemporaries of the translators. Therefore to my mind it is less probable that such a translation goes back to a different *Vorlage*[18].

---

16 For a study of the double readings in the Septuagint cf. Z. Talshir, "Double Translations in the Septuagint". In *VI Congress of the International Organization for Septuagint and Cognate Studies* Atlanta, Georgia 1987, p. 21-63. Many of the remarks made there are valid for the Old Latin too: doublets as a result of alternative readings; both translate the same Hebrew word and the copyist did not want to renounce to any of the meanings; doublets as a result of intentional creation or as the result of an exegetical process.
In my opinion the literary elaboration in this passage of the Old Latin is so strong that it can hardly be claimed that it goes back to a Vorlage near to the Old Greek and consequently to the Hebrew as stated by J. Trebolle, "Crítica textual de 1 Re 22,35. Aportación de una nueva lectura de la *Vetus Latina*". *Sefarad* 52, 1 (1992) 235-243.
17 L. Koehler-W. Baumgartner, *Lexicon in Veteris Testamenti Libros*, Leiden 1985 and F. Cantera-M. Iglesias, *Sagrada Biblia*, Madrid BAC 1979[2].
18 Other examples with similar characteristics in 1 Sam 1,6 and 2 Kings 2,12.

b) Intentional changes of interpretation.

In some passages the reason for a different translation cannot be attributed to difficulty in understanding the text, but theological or midrashic considerations, or even stylistic reasons for the change can be detected:

12.—1 Sam 17,4 (concerning Goliath's size): *Altitudo illius cubitorum sex et decem palmarum latitudo eius*

Ant: ὕψος αὐτοῦ τεσσάρων πηχῶν καὶ σπιθαμῆς

MT: נבהו שש אמות וזרת

V: Altitudinis sex cubitorum et palmo.

His height was six (four in the LXX, Josephus and 4QSam[a]) cubits and a span.

The LXX translator shortened already Goliath's height from six to four cubits[19], in order to lessen the fantastic character of this figure in the Hebrew. But the addition of the Old Latin, without support in the known manuscripts or versions, constitutes a typical example of literary initiative, due to either the translator or to one of the later copyists. The second part of the verse was probably generated from a word such as *palmus*, a complementary fraction taken to be an appendix to the text ("altitudo illius cubitorum sex et palmi" in a possible intermediate stage of the tradition). In order to complement the information and clarify the meaning a creative copyist transformed the last word into a new sentence describing Goliath's width[20]. In any case the author of this addition has shown enough literary and stylistic ability as to frame a sentence with chiastic structure, a common stylistic device in Greco-roman rethoric. And this is not the only trace of literary elaboration in the Old Latin[21].

13.—2 Kings 5,8 (Elisha says to Naaman): *Veniat nunc ad me et cognosces quoniam est Deus in Israel, et ego propheta eius.*

---

[19] A part of the LXX tradition (mss N and several minuscles) read πέντε, while the Hexaplaric recension and other group of minuscles read ἕξ, cf. Brooke-McLean-Thackeray, *The Old Testament in Greek*, II/I, p. 55.

[20] See in S. Talshir, "Double Translations in the Septuagint", p. 47-51, other examples of a new sentence created from a double reading or a divergent variant in the Septuagint.

[21] Cf. J. Trebolle Barrera, "Reflejos de paralelismo hebreo en la Vetus Latina". *Sefarad* 46, 1-2 (1986) 463-471.

Ant: παραγενέσθω δὴ πρὸς μὲ Νεεμάν, καὶ γνώσεται ὅτι ἔστι προφήτης ἐν Ἰσραήλ.

MT: יבא נא אלי וידע כי יש נביא בישראל

V: Veniat ad me et sciat esse prophetam in Israhel.

Let him come to me and he will learn that there is a prophet in
Israel.

The starting point of this expansion was probably an alternative
reading already present in the Hebrew[22]. Instead of נביא some
manuscripts read אלהים[23]. But from this doublet or alternative
reading, unknown in the Greek tradition, the Old Latin rearranges
the whole sentence by introducing a set of changes: the omission of
Naaman, the substitution of the third person for the second one (*cognosces*) connecting it with the king of Israel instead of with Naaman;
a full development of the second part of the sentence creating a new
meaning: it is the king of Israel and not Naaman who has to know
that there is a God in Israel and that Elisha is his prophet. There is
no special difficulty in the translation of this sentence. The changes
originated in all probability from a primitive alternative reading
(*propheta / deus*) already attested in the Hebrew, but lost in the Greek
tradition. The Old Latin shows a great creativity able to transform
the doublet into a new sentence with a new, theologically oriented,
meaning.

c) Divergent readings produced by a mixture of different phenomena (double translation plus corruption; perplexing translation plus
corruption etc.)

14.—1 Sam 5,4: *Et caput Dagon et ambae palmae manuum eius, et ambo
vestigia (vestigie codd) eius ablatae erant per partes centum.*

Ant: καὶ ἡ κεφαλὴ Δαγὼν καὶ ἀμφότερα τὰ ἴχνη τῶν ποδῶν αὐτοῦ
ἀφῃρημένα ἐπὶ τὰ ἐμπρόσθια τῶν σταθμῶν [+ ἔκαστοι Ba₂: +
ἔκαστον AN rell]

---

[22] Cf. S. Talmon, *Conflate Readings (OT)*. *IDBS*, Nashville 1982[3] and ——,
"Double Readings in the Massoretic Text". *Textus* 1 (1961) 144-183.

[23] Ms 125 of Kennicott, cf. B. Kennicott, *Vetus Testamentum Hebraicum cum variis
Lectionibus*, Oxonii 1776 and J.-B. De Rossi, *Variae Lectiones Veteris Testamenti. Vol.
II*, Parmae 1785. This variant reading was known by Chrysostom too, *Chry. lap.*,
1,656: "Mitte, inquit, ad me: mitte Naaman syrum: ut sciat quia *deus* est in
Israel".

MT: וראש דגון ושתי כפות ידיו כרתות אל המפתן

V: Caput autem Dagon et duae palmae manuum eius abscisae erant super limen.

Dagon's head and both his hands were broken off upon the threshold.

In the Old Latin the double reading *ambae palmae / ambo vestigia* resulted from a double translation of the Greek ἴχνη that means 'track, footstep' and 'palms of the hands' (a *hapax* in this passage of the Septuagint according to Liddell-Scott-Jones Greek dictionary)[24]. On the other hand it is not difficult to surmise behind the reading *centum* a corruption at the level of the Greek *Vorlage*, that is, at the level of the translation itself. Thus the Latin translator read in all probability ἑκατόν instead of ἕκαστον transmitted by most of the manuscritps[25]. In any case, again the resultant meaning of the Old Latin translation is quite different from that of the original. In this case the Old Latin doublet tries to harmonize the reading of Antiochene with the reading of the majority Septuagint.

15.—2 Kings 16,9: *Audito nuntio... Et cepit eam, et comprehendit Core et Ason reges eius.*

Ant: καὶ ἤκουσεν... καὶ συνέλαβεν αὐτήν, καὶ ἀπῴκισε τὴν πόλιν καὶ τὸν Ῥαασσὼν ἐθανάτωσεν.

MT: וישמע אליו מלך אשור ויעל מלך אשור אל דמשק ויתפשה ויגלה
קירה ואת רצין המית

V: Qui et adquievit... et vastavit eam et transtulit habitatores eius Cyrenen, Rasin autem interfecit.

The king of Assyria responded to his plea and proceeded against Damascus. He captured it and exiled it to Kir and put Rezin to death.

The geographical and historical distance of the translators from the original had already transformed the locativ קירה—the city of Kir probably situated in Mesopotamia—into *Cyrenen*, a city on the coast of North Africa (cf. Vulgate and Targum (לקרינא) and part of the

---

[24] The Old Latin follows here the majority Septuagint, not the Antiochene text, which reads τὰ ἴχνη χειρῶν αὐτοῦ like the Masoretic Text.

[25] See other examples in 1 Kings 20,16; 20,19; 2 Kings 3,4 mentioned above and 23,4.

Hexaplaric tradition (κυρήνηνδε following Aquila)[26]. We do not know what the original translation of the VL was, but we can reconstruct its early transmission as follows: the copyist meets *Core* in the text, no doubt a transcription of the Hebrew קירה[27]. The other noun *Ason* comes from a corruption of the Greek tradition (Josephus-ed has αρασην) from the Hebrew *Rezin*. Obviously the hardly known city of Kir[28] can be easily transformed into Core, a new king of Damascus, creating a new meaning far different both from the original and from the other versions, including the Targum.

16.—1 Kings 20,8-9: *Ne audieris verba ei sed nec voluntatem tuam ostendas illi[9], et confortatus rex dixit nuntiis filii Ader:*

Ant (21, 8-9): Μὴ ἀκούσῃς καὶ μὴ θελήσῃς[9]. καὶ εἶπεν ὁ βασιλεὺς Ἰσραὴλ τοῖς ἀγγέλοις υἱοῦ Ἀδέρ

MT: אל תשמע ולוא תאבה [9]ויאמר למלאכי בן הדד

V: Non audias neque adquiescas illi[9], respondit itaque nuntiis Benadad.

Do not listen or agree[9]. So he said to the envoys of Benhadad.

This is a good example of the development of a text, making explicit the implicit, which has already started with the Antiochene text. This text tends to fill out the information by adding the subject (proper noun or pronoun) of the second sentence. It is possible—althougth we lack the evidence in the collection of variants transmitted by Kennicott and De Rossi—that the Greek translator knew an alternative reading in the Hebrew (מלך next to למלאכי). The VL develops the first sentence still further by adding the complements of the two Greek verbs, and inserts in addition the midrashic gloss *confortatus*.

17.—1 Kings 21,27: *Sed super hoc verbo paenituit Achab et reveritus est a facie Domini, et ibat plorans scissis vestibus suis, et operuit se cilicio et erat indutus cilicio in die illo et paenituit ex die qua percussit Nabathaeum.*

---

[26] Cf. A. Sperber, *The Bible in Aramaic. II The Former Prophets* and Brooke-McLean-Thackeray, *The Old Testament in Greek*, ad locum.

[27] By the way, in the light of the Septuagint translation Montgomery-Gehman think that קירה is probably a gloss to signal the fulfilment of the prophecy in Amos 9,7, cf. J.A. Montgomery—H.S. Gehman, *A Critical and Exegetical Commentary on the Books of Kings*, Edinburgh 1951, p. 459.

[28] "The location of this place is still an enigma", cf. Cogan-Tadmor, *II Kings*, p. 188.

Ant (20,27): ἀλλ' ὑπὲρ τοῦ λόγου ὡς κατενύχθη 'Αχαὰβ ἀπὸ προσώπου Κυρίου, καὶ ἐπορεύθη κλαίων καὶ διέρρηξε τὸν χιτῶνα αὐτοῦ καὶ ἐζώσατο σάκκον ἐπὶ τὸ σῶμα αὐτοῦ καὶ ἐνήστευσε καὶ περιεβάλετο σάκκον ἐν τῇ ἡμέρᾳ ᾗ ἐπάταξεν 'Ιεζάβελ Ναβουθαί, ... ἐγένετο ῥῆμα Κυρίου...

MT: ויהי כשמע אחאב את הדברים האלה ויקרע בגדיו וישם שק על בשרו ויצום וישכב בשק ויהלך אט

V: Itaque cum audisset Ahab sermones istos scidit vestem suam et operuit cilicio carnem suam ieiunavitque et dormivit in sacco et ambulabat dimisso capite.

And it happened that, when Ahab heard these words, he tore his clothes and put sackcloth on his body and fasted, and lay in sackcloth and went about quietly.

The Greek has already re-arranged the sequence of the narrative and has made an addition at the end of the verse. Obviously the Old Latin follows the Antiochene text, which is far in this passage from the Masoretic Text (see the major additions καὶ ἐπορεύθη κλαίων and ἐν τῇ ἡμέρᾳ—Ναβουθαί). Furthermore in the Old Latin traces of double translations for the same Greek word can be detected (*paenituit / reveritus est* for κατενύχθη and *in die illo / ex die qua* for ἐν τῇ ἡμέρᾳ ᾗ), as well as other signs of a free treatment of the *Vorlage* (omission of ἐπὶ τὸ σῶμα—ἐνήστευσεν). The result is a new sentence twice as long as the Hebrew original and with quite a different meaning. Nevertheless I think it is possible to explain the Old Latin text as a new redactional arrangement on the Antiochene without recourse to a different *Vorlage*.

18.—1 Kings 20,39: *Cum exissem ego, servus tuus, tecum in militiam ad belligerandum, et ecce homo introduxit ad me quendam virum ex hostibus, et dixit mihi: Custodi mihi hunc; si autem exiliens fugerit a te, anima tua pro anima illius; nam si servaveris eum, talentum argenti constituo tibi in mercedem.*

Ant (21,39): καὶ ἐγένετο ὡς ὁ βασιλεὺς παρεπορεύετο, καὶ αὐτὸς ἐβόα πρὸς τὸν βασιλέα καὶ εἶπεν ὁ δοῦλός σου ἐξῆλθεν ἐπὶ τὴν στρατιὰν τοῦ πολεμεῖν καὶ ἰδοὺ ἀνὴρ εἰξήγαγε πρὸς μὲ ἄνδρα καὶ εἶπε μοι Φύλαξόν μοι τοῦτον. καὶ ἔσται ἐὰν ἐκπηδῶν ἐκπηδήσῃ ἔσται ἡ ψυχή σου ἀντὶ τῆς ψυχῆς αὐτοῦ, ἢ τάλαντον ἀργυρίου στήσεις.

MT: ויהי המלך עבר והוא צעק אל המלך ויאמר עבדך יצא בקרב המלחמה והנה איש סר ויבא אלי איש ויאמר שמר את האיש הזה

אִם הִפָּקֵד יִפָּקֵד וְהָיְתָה נַפְשְׁךָ תַּחַת נַפְשׁוֹ אוֹ כִכַּר כֶּסֶף תִּשְׁקוֹל

V: Cumque rex transiret clamavit ad regem et ait: servus tuus egressus est ad proeliandum comminus, cumque fugisset vir unus adduxit eum quidam ad me et ait: custodi virum istum qui si lapsus fuerit erit anima tua pro anima eius aut talentum argenti adpendes.

And as the king was passing he cried out to the king and said, Your servant went forth into the thick of the battle and there came a man, who turned aside and brought a man to me and said Keep this man. If he is missing your life shall be forfeit for his life or you shall pay out a talent.

The text of the Old Latin condenses the first part of the verse through profound changes in the structure of the sentence: omission of the sentence about the king; subordination with *cum historicum*; introduction of the first person instead of the 3rd found in the original narrative and the other versions. Finally, the explanatory addition of *ex hostibus*, and, more important, the transformation of the last sentence—too obscure and concise in the original—into a more intelligible one, but with a completely different meaning. Once again these changes are not evidence for a different *Vorlage* but bear witness to an intense redactional activity by the translator in comparison with the Hebrew original, the LXX or the text of the Vulgate[29].

19.—2 Kings 13,17b (according to L₁₁₅): *Et percuties Syriam in Aseroth quae est contra faciem Samariae usque at finem. Et aperuit fenestram secundam et dixit sagittare et sagittavit sagittam salutis Domini et sagittam salutis Israel et dixit Helisseus Percuties Syriam totam.*

Ant (v. 16): βέλος σωτηρίας τῷ κυρίῳ καὶ βέλος σωτηρίας ἐν Ἰσραήλ, καὶ πατάξεις τὴν Συρίαν ἐν Ἀφὲκ ἕως συντελείας

MT: חֵץ תְּשׁוּעָה לַיהוה וְחֵץ תְּשׁוּעָה בַאֲרָם וְהִכִּיתָ אֶת אֲרָם בַּאֲפֵק עַד כַּלֵּה

V: Sagitta salutis Domini et sagitta salutis contra Syriam percutiesque Syriam in Afec donec consumas eam.

An arrow of victory for Yahveh. An arrow of victory over Aram. You will defeat Aram at Aphek completely.

At first sight it may appear that this text from the *Palimpsestus Vindobonensis* goes back to the original stratum of the passage. The sym-

---

[29] See other examples in 1 Kings 22,30; 2 Kings 4,28; 5,1; 10,32; 12,9 and 19,24.

bolic action ordered by the prophet Elisha, based on the ancient magic practice of belomancy is supported by similar repetitions of the rite in vv. 18-19. On the other hand the absence of this repetition in the Hebrew and Greek texts could be explained through parablepsis due to homoioteleuton (Συρίαν... Συρίαν in the Greek, or ארם... ארם in the Hebrew). Nevertheless, despite this appearance of originality, this addition is probably of secondary character too; this can be detected from the double translation of the last two words of the Greek (ἕως συντέλειας) in this verse: *usque at finem* and *totam*. The first part of the verse (2 Kings 13,17a) has been translated literally in *Palimpsestus Vindobonensis* from the Antiochene text. But when the copyist found *Aseroth* (probably a corruption of the Greek Συρίαν ἐν 'Αφέκ) he had problems of identification and introduced the gloss *quae est contra faciem Samariae*[30] (cf. v. 13,6). Moreover the *Palimpsestus Vindobonensis* is the only witness of the Old Latin recording this expansion.

---

[30] Cf. Cogan-Tadmor, *II Kings*, p. 148.

CHAPTER SIX

DIFFERENT *VORLAGE* OR SECONDARY
DEVELOPMENT? THE ENIGMA OF THE OLD LATIN

I have just analysed a set of Old Latin singular readings that could
be explained with more or less plausibility, as the consequences of
a peculiar translation technique, perhaps not as literal as has been
thought of, or as the result of a complex text transmission through
the *strata* of three different languages. In the first series of instances
I detected the frequency of double readings as a characteristic of the
Old Latin of Kings, that follows, and sometimes develops further,
this feature of its main *Vorlage*, the Antiochene text. I presented
several instances of double sentences too, generated from conflated
readings that needed to be harmonised.

A second set of Old Latin variants could be attributed to diverse
accidents in the transmission of the text, that, as a translation, has
its starting point in the Hebrew, but goes on through the Greek
version, especially in the form of the Antiochene text, to the Latin
transmission itself. Traces of palaeographic corruption that influenced the Old Latin modifying its text can be detected in all these
three stages.

Finally a third set of singular readings seemed to have originated
from the midrashic glosses and exegetical commentaries produced
for difficult passages, or from doubtful translations, and intentional
changes brought about by a combination of different phenomena:
corruption plus interpretation, corruption plus alternative readings,
etc. . . and the need to re-arrange the sentence in order to make
sense within the new context.

We noticed too the difficulty of typifying the VL aberrant texts in
Kings. Very often the Old Latin expands a concise expression in its
Vorlage in order to smooth the meaning, but it sometimes condenses too when it has to deal with repetition or a cumbersome sentence in the Antiochene. Usualy the VL translates very literaly even
following the word order of the Greek syntax rather than the Latin.
But it also shows considerable signs of free reworking, remoulding
a sentence with the insertion of stylistic figures that are lacking in
its Vorlage.

Let us now take a step forward in our inquiry about the enigma of
the Old Latin. After a few instances of readings for which we cannot
surmise any other reason than the free reshaping of the sentence,
I will focus on a group of readings especially connected with the
original Hebrew. They have a particular interest because it must be
stressed that the language of the glosses, in spite of the accidents of
transmission mentioned above, corresponds to the Latin common
between the end of the 2nd century and the end of the 3rd century
A.D.[1]

20.—1 Kings 21,19: *Occidisti Nabutheum ut in pretium sanguinis possideres vineam eius.*
Ant (20,19): ἐφόνευσας καὶ ἐκληρονόμησας
MT: הרצחת וגם ירשת
V: Occidisti insuper et possedisti.
Have you done murder and moreover taken possesion?

The verse has been re-arranged by the VL which inserts this sentence in the middle of the narrative, being at the beginning in the
Greek and the Hebrew[2]. In contrast with the two verbs joined by
the preposition 'and' in the Greek and in the Hebrew, no doubt an
example of concision, the VL transforms the second verb into a
subordinate clause and makes explicit the content that was implicit
in such a *locutio praegnans*[3].

21.—2 Kings 10,11-10: *Nam eradicabo universos qui relicti sunt in domo
Achab in Israel et omnes cognatos eius, et propinquos eius*[10] *ut sciant cuncti
quia non cadent verba domini in terra, quae locutus est de domo Achab in manu
Heliae.*
Ant (2 Kings 10,10-11): ἴδετε ὅτι οὐ πεσεῖται ἀπὸ τῶν λόγων

---

[1] Cf. C. Morano, *Glosas marginales*, p. LXXXI and A. Moreno, *Las glosas marginales*, p. 407-408.

[2] Cf. A. Moreno, *Las glosas marginales*, p. 206-207. The majority Septuagint prefix ὡς σύ.

[3] The same could be said of the following sentence in 2 Kings 5,12-13: "Et haec dicens regiravit se abiens in iracundia. [13] *Et ut venit ad Jordanem* servi illius...". The first sentence of v. 13 is missing in all the known manuscript tradition. Nevertheless it fits the sequence of the narrative. It seems to have being inserted by the Old Latin *ad sensum* following the ancient technique of the *Wiederaufnahme*. Likewise 2 Kings 7,6: *Deus enim misericors Israel*, missing from the rest of the tradition. It may belong to the original version, but it looks like a pious gloss of the translator.

Κυρίου ἐπὶ τὴν γῆν ὧν ἐλάλησε κατὰ τοῦ οἴκου ᾿Αχαάβ. καὶ ἐποίησε Κύριος ὅσα ἐλάλησεν ἐν χειρὶ τοῦ δούλου αὐτοῦ ᾿Ηλίου.[11] καὶ ἐπάταξεν ᾿Ιοὺ πάντας τοὺς καταλειφθέντας ἐν τῷ οἴκῳ ᾿Αχαὰβ ἐν ᾿Ιεζραὴλ καὶ πάντας τοὺς ἀγχιστεύοντας αὐτοῦ καὶ πάντας τοὺς γνωστοὺς αὐτοῦ καὶ τοὺς ἱερεῖς αὐτοῦ καὶ τοὺς ἁδροὺς αὐτοῦ ἕως τοῦ μὴ καταλειφθῆναι αὐτοῦ κατάλειμμα.

This sentence in the *Vetus Latina* shows some agreement with the Antiochene, but the re-arrangement is so profound—change of order in the verses, changes of subject and person, subordination, several omissions, all without support in the known manuscripts—that it looks as if the whole narrative has been re-written in order to emphasize that no word of the Lord will fail. Although the inversion of vv. 10 and 11 may point to the possibility that the whole sentence is based on a different *Vorlage*, some incongruities of the narrative in the Old Latin as well as the different interpretations of the Greek lead one to think rather of an exegetical commentary, added to stress the general statemenet ''sciant cuncti quia non cadent verba domini in terra''[4].

22.—2 Kings 19,3: *Dies tribulationis hodie in me sicut dies doloris descenderunt usque ad genua mea, et virtus non est parienti.*

Ant: ῾Ημέρα θλίψεως καὶ ὀνειδισμοῦ καὶ ἐλεγμοῦ καὶ παροργισμοῦ ἡ ἡμέρα αὕτη, ὅτι ἦλθον οἱ υἱοὶ ἕως ὠδίνων, καὶ οὐκ ἔστιν ἰσχὺς τῇ τικτούσῃ.

MT: יום צרה ותוכחה ונאצה היום הזה כי באו בנים עד משבר וכח אין ללדה

V: Dies tribulationis et increpationis et blasphemiae dies iste, venerunt filii usque ad partum et vires non habet parturiens.

This day is a day of distress, of rebuke and of contempt. 'Children have come to the breach; but there is no strenght for the birth'.

We have for this passage another witness of the Old Latin under the sigla *Al.* This second version translates literally: «Dies tribulationis et improperii (et) odii, quoniam intraverunt filii hodie usque ad parentes (perhaps corruption for ''parietes''?), et virtus non est parturientis». Certainly if one compares this second version with the first, one realises that the second is much more literal. The first ver-

---

4 Cf. A. Moreno, *Las glosas marginales*, p. 211-212.

sion of the Old Latin condenses the narrative and gives a different meaning, using *genua mea* as a euphemism of ὠδίνων and removing the reference to the 'sons' while maintaining the image of child-birth[5]. But it is quite possible that the mention of the knees in the Old Latin goes back to a different reading of the Hebrew משברוכה in *scriptio continua*[6] leading to a false division of the words (= ברכי, *genua mea*). The presence of this alternative reading may have generated the remoulding of the whole sentence. In any case this is a typical example of the problem we are dealing with: are we to suppose different texts or corrupt texts? Do these readings go back to a different *Vorlage* or are they due to the literary activity of the translators or early copyists?

23.—1 Kings 22,30 (The king of Israel said to Jehoshaphat of Juda): *Da mihi vestimentum tuum et sic introibo in bellum, et tu vestite vestimentum meum; et factum est ut commutatis inter se vestimentis intrarent in pugnam.*

Ant: Συγκαλύψομαι καὶ εἰσελεύσομαι εἰς τὸν πόλεμον, καὶ σὺ ἔνδυσαι τὸν ἱματισμόν μου. καὶ συνεκαλύψατο ὁ βασιλεὺς Ἰσραὴλ καὶ εἰσῆλθεν εἰς τὸν πόλεμον.

TM: התחפש ובא במלחמה ואתה לבש בנדיך ויתחפש מלך ישראל ויבוא במלחמה

V: Sume arma et ingredere proelium et induere vestibus tuis. Porro rex Israhel mutavit habitum et ingressus est bellum.

I will disguise myself to go into the battle, but you shall wear your royal robes. So he went into the battle in disguise.

The Old Latin seems to be a free translation of the Greek that translates the Hebrew literally with only the change of the suffix of the first person for that of the second. This change occurs in the Syriac version and in the Targum too, and in all probability goes back to a different Hebrew *Vorlage*.

24.—2 Kings 4,28 (The Shunammite woman replies to Elisha, the man of God): *Si poposci filium a domino, non sic poposci sicut tu fecisti: et ecce ibi hic mortuus est.*

---

[5] On the connection of the knees with the throes of childbirth in Greek literature cf. Euripides, *Phoenissae* 355: αἱ δι' ὠδίνων γοναί.

[6] On this kind of mistakes in Hebrew cf. Weingreen, *Introduction*, p. 50.

Ant: Μὴ ᾐτησάμην υἱὸν παρὰ τοῦ κυρίου; οὐχὶ σὺ πεποίηκας; οὐκ εἶπον Οὐ πλανήσεις μετ' ἐμοῦ;

MT: השאלתי בן מאת אדני הלא אמרתי לא תשלה אתי

V: Nunquid petivi filium a domino meo, nunquid non dixi tibi ne inludas me?

Did I ask for a son of my Lord? Did I not say, 'Do not deceive me'?

The sentence has been fully remoulded in the Old Latin which bases itself on the Antiochene, because in *fecisti* one can recognize the πεποίηκας of the Greek. But the sense has been totally changed syntactically as well as stylistically. Again this looks like a stylistic re-writing of the sentence rather than a translation of a different *Vorlage*.

We turn now to the corruptions or alternative readings which arose at the stage of the Hebrew *Vorlage* and that cannot be explained at the other stages of the Greek or Latin transmission. My claim is that these readings, being rooted in the Hebrew, are very old; I do not mean that the Old Latin translators took them directly from the Hebrew. Probably those readings came to them through their Greek *Vorlage* or one of the later translators, but whithin the traditions known to us, their genesis can be explained only from the Hebrew.

It is well known that the Old Latin (as well as the Antiochene) maintains the composite name of Baʿal (instead of *Bošet*), which is prior to the corrections of the scribes[7]. In 1 Kings 21,10 the Old Latin again bears witness to a text prior to the emendations of the scribes: *Maledixit Nabuthae Deum et regem*, against the Vulgate (*benedixit*), backed by the Greek and the Hebrew, that has no sense in the context and was employed as a euphemism to avoid the name of God being close to the verb קלל. Only the Targum and the Peshitta support the reading of the Old Latin which is probably the original[8].

---

[7] For the emendations of the scribes and the so-called *tiqqune soferim*, cf. C.D. Ginsburg, *Introduction to the Massoretico-Critical Edition of the Hebrew Bible. Prolegomenon by H.M. Orlinsky*, New York 1966, 400-401. Cf. 2 Sam 2,8; 9,10; 23,8 etc.

[8] Cf. Ginsburg, *Introduction*, 367. This euphemism is frequent at the beginning of the Book of Job. Only ὁ ἑβραῖος to Job 2,5 translates the ברך of the Masoretic Text by βλασφημέω, in contrast with the Septuagint translation by εὐλογέω, and the tame circumlocution εἰπόν τι ῥῆμα εἰς Κύριον at Job 2,9e, cf. C. Cox, "Vocabulary for Wrongdoing and Forgiveness in the Greek Translations of Job". *Textus* XV (1990) 119-130, p. 124.

Traces of a different reading of the Masoretic Text, lost in the rest of the tradition, can be divined also in the Old Latin reading *ad regem Syriae* (2 Kings 3,26) where the other witnesses read Edom[9]. This evidence of contacts with a pre-hexaplaric Hebrew text was already detected by Brock for the Lucianic recension[10]. Therefore this phenomenon is well known in the Antiochene text which constitutes the main basis of the Old Latin translation in the Historical books[11].

To my mind, another proof that the Old Latin translators (as represented in the marginal glosses) were in contact with a Hebrew tradition lost in the known Greek manuscripts is provided by the sporadic Hebrew transliterations preserved in the Old Latin where the LXX translates[12].

Let us examine now in detail some more Old Latin variants probably connected with a different Hebrew *Vorlage*:

25.—2 Kings 2,12 (Elisha's crying to Elijah when taken up to the heaven): *Agitator Israel cui me dereliquisti.*

Ant: ἅρμα Ἰσραὴλ καὶ ἱππεὺς αὐτοῦ

MT: רכב ישראל ופרשיו

V: Pater mi pater mi currus Israhel et auriga eius.

My father, my father! The chariots of Israel and its horsemen.

Probably the Old Latin translator relies on a reading *rokeb*, participle of *rakab* = "to ride an animal or a chariot". The word *agitator* cannot be linked with *parasaw* = horsemen (*auriga* in the Vulgate), because

---

[9] Due to the confusion between *res* and *dalet*, mentioned above, cf. Weingreen, *Introduction*, p. 38-40.

[10] S.P. Brock, *The Recensions of the Septuagint Versions of 1 Samuel*, Diss. Oxford 1966, p. 175: "L in particular appear to contain certain approximations *not* deriving from the fith column: many of these are taken from other columns of the Hexapla, notably Symmachus, but a few are totally unconnected with the Hexapla, and some of these even go back to a variant Hebrew text (and so in all probability represent a very early *stratum* of approximations)".

[11] "Numerous Antiochian readings are originated by an alternative reading of the Masoretic text, without connection with the Hexapla, readings that represent in all probability a very early stratum of Ant", cf. N. Fernández Marcos, "Literary and Editorial Features of the Antiochian Text in Kings". In *VI Congress of the International Organization for Septuagint and Cognate Studies*, ed. by Claude Cox, Atlanta Georgia 1987, 287-304, p. 298 with examples in note 39. See also S. Talmon, "Synonymous readings in the Textual Tradition of the Old Testament". *Studies in the Bible, Scripta Hierosolymitana VIII*, Jerusalem 1961, p. 335-383.

[12] Cf. *chremel zecalin* (2 Kings 4,42); *paradrin* (2 Kings 5,17); *gaphela* (2 Kings 5,24); *mascarath, mechonot, cyrot* (2 Kings 16,17); *messelat* (2 Kings 18,17) etc.

in 2 Kings 13,14 the Old Latin repeats *agitator Israel et dux eius* (that is, 'dux' employed for the Hebrew *parasaw!*). Furthermore in 2 Kings 9,25, a text whose corruption (already detected by Vercellone), gives a meaning totally different from that of the Greek, Hebrew or Vulgate[13], all we can say is that the Old Latin again gives *agitator* for the same Hebrew root רכבים present as a doublet behind *qui ascendebat* (Greek ἐπιβεβηκότες) too.

The second part or the verse, *cui me dereliquisti*, probably translates the first meaning of *paras* = 'divide', 'separate', instead of the second one 'horseman', 'cart-horse' (in Luther's Bible 'Gespann').

26.—2 Kings 9,23: *Et circumagens Ioram currum suum dixit ad Ochoziam: Iaculare, Ochozia!*

Ant: καὶ ἐπέστρεψεν Ἰωρὰμ τὰς χεῖρας αὐτοῦ τοῦ φυγεῖν, καὶ εἶπε πρὸς Ὀχοζείαν Δόλος Ὀχοζεία.

MT: ויהפך יהורם ידיו וינס ויאמר אל אחזיהו מרמה אחזיה

V: Convertit autem Ioram manum suam et fugiens ait ad Ahaziam: insidiae Ahazia.

Joram turned his hands and fled, and he said to Ahaziah, 'Treason, Ahaziah!'.

I consider unlikely the possibility of a palaeographic corruption at the stage of the Latin transmission or at the stage of the Greek leading to *iaculare* instead of "treason". On the other hand the original reading is not so rare as to cause problems to the translator. Δόλος is translated regularly in the Old Latin by 'insidiose' or 'sub dolo'[14]. Consequently the word *iaculare* probably arose as translation of τοξεύειν, an alternative Greek reading that understood מרמה = 'treason' as a derivative of ירה = 'shoot' whose equivalent in Greek for the *hifil* is precisely τοξεύειν. Therefore, the Septuagint translator understood its *Vorlage* as a derivative of ירה or of רמה = 'to throw'. The possibility cannot be excluded of a different *Vorlage* connected with some of these Hebrew roots

---

[13] *Quoniam memini ego agitatorem meum elemedab retulisse qui ascendebat post Achab patrem eius, quod dominus deus suscitavit super eum praedestinatum prophetam dicentem verba domini.*

The Masoretic Text reads: "Remember how you and I were riding side by side behind Ahab, his father, when Yahveh made this pronouncement about him".

[14] Cf. A.V. Billen, *The Old Latin Texts of the Heptateuch*, Cambridge 1927, p. 201.

27.—1 Sam 11,5: *Et ecce Saul ibat mane post boves in agro, et vidit omnes plorantes.*

Ant: καὶ ἰδοὺ Σαοὺλ ἤρχετο πρωῒ κατόπισθεν τῶν βοῶν ἐξ ἀγροῦ.

MT: וחנה שאול בא אחרי הבקר מן השׂדה

V: Et ecce Saul veniebat sequens boves de agro.

Now just at that time Saul was coming in behind the oxen from the field.

The first part of the verse is a conflated translation of הבקר to be found in the MT and behind the LXX (according to *Codex Vaticanus*: μετὰ τῷ πρωί) which read the same consonantal text with different vocalization (*baqar / boqer*). This double reading had been already harmonised in the Antiochene[15]. From the Antiochene text it passed to the Old Latin. The linking sentence "et vidit omnes plorantes" is a good connection between the end of v. 4 "all the people began to weep aloud" and the following question of v. 5 "Why are the people weeping?". Therefore it could have stood in the original, as an example of the literary technique of composition called *Wiederaufnahme*. But given the tendency of the Old Latin to explain and fill out the narrative, smoothing the ruptures of meaning, it seems more probable that it has been created by the translator. Besides, there is no trace of this sentence having fallen out because of homoioteleuton in the Hebrew[16], neither is it probable that it could have arisen because of corruption or because of a different reading of the *Vorlage*.

28.—1 Sam 17,53: *Et reversi sunt viri Israel comburentes post alienigenas et conculcantes castra eorum.*

Ant: καὶ ἀνέστρεψαν ἄνδρες Ἰσραὴλ ἐκκαίοντες (cod. ἐκκλί-νοντες) ὀπίσω τῶν ἀλλοφύλων, καὶ προενόμευσαν τὰς παρεμβολὰς αὐτῶν.

MT: וישבו בני ישראל מדלק אחרי פלשתים וישסו את־מחניהם

V: Et revertentes filii Israhel postquam persecuti fuerant Philisteos invaserunt castra eorum.

When the Israelites returned from their pursuit of the Philistines, they looted their camp.

---

[15] Cf. N. Fernández Marcos, "Literary and Editorial Features of the Antiochian Text in Kings", p. 297.

[16] In Hebrew it would stand as וירא כל העם בכים.

No doubt this reading of the Old Latin gives the original in agreement with the Masoretic Hebrew מדלק אחרי פלשתים. Not only that but, as Skehan remarked[17] this reading of the Old Latin can also help to restore the original Septuagint, which was probably corrupted through the text transmission from ἐκκαίοντες, with no support in the manuscripts, to ἐκκλίνοντες preserved in the whole tradition.

29.—1 Sam 25,6: *Multis annis salvus sis et tu et domus tua, et omnia tua salva sint.*

May you have peace! May your house have peace!. May all that is yours have peace!.

The Hebrew כה לחי ואתה is understood by the Greek translator as τάδε εἰς ὥρας καὶ σὺ ὑγιαίνων... "for the fitting time to you" or "hurrah for you"[18]. The Vulgate translates "sic fratribus meis et tibi", 'to my brothers and you' reading *le'ehay*. There is no Hebrew variant in the medieval manuscripts collected by Kennicott and De Rossi which supports the reading of the Old Latin. But if we take into account that this variant reading is confirmed by other witnesses of the VL (such as Weber's interpolations to Samuel[19]), and above all, that it is also attested by Josephus who reads ἐπ' ἔτη πολλά (*Ant.* VI, 297), the probability increases that the VL has preserved here an ancient reading lost in the rest of the tradition (except for Josephus). Nevertheless as the other versions (Peshitta, Targum) seem to share the obscure reading of the MT לחי, "to the one who lives?" (pausal form of *lahay*, so Driver), Old Latin and Josephus may point to a common elaboration which interpreted the Hebrew word in the same temporal sense already suggested by the Septuagint.

30.—2 Sam 5,6 (The Jebusites say to David): *Tanta est, inquiunt, civitas ut a debilibus arcearis, ad quos David respondit: facite, inquiens, et ego iubeam ut parva sublimia tangant et exeat inde proverbium.*

---

[17] Cf. P.W. Skehan, "Turning or Burning? 1 Sam 17:53 LXX". *CBQ* 38 (1976) 193-195.

[18] Cf. a similar expression ε]ὶς ὥρας πᾶσι τοῖς τὴν πόλιν φιλοῦσιν in *POxy. 41.29* (III/IV A.D.).

[19] "Hæc multis annis facias salvus tu et domus tua et omnia tua", cf. R. Weber, "Les interpolations du livre de Samuel dans les manuscrits de la Vulgate". *Miscellanea G. Mercati 1, ST 121*, Vatican 1946, p. 19-39.

Ant: ἐρρέθη Οὐκ εἰσελεύσῃ ὧδε, διότι ἀπέστησαν οἱ χωλοὶ καὶ οἱ τυφλοὶ λέγοντες Οὐκ εἰσελεύσεται Δαυὶδ ὧδε.

MT: לאמר לא תבוא הוה כי אם הסירך העורים והפסחים לאמר לא
יבוא דוד הנה

V: Non ingredieris huc nisi abstuleris caecos et claudos dicentes non ingredietur David huc.

You shall not come in here!. (For the blind and the lame had incited them, saying, 'David shall not come in here!').

This text is not transmitted by L_{91-95}[20], but by two other VL witnesses: Weber's interpolations to Samuel[21] and *ms Germ 11* according to Sabatier. The passage constitutes an ancient *crux interpretum*. It has no sense in Hebrew, and the attempts to explain the origin of the proverb remain obscure. McCarter devotes some pages to this verse, but he does not comment on the Old Latin[22]. The scanty remains from Qumran (4QSam[a]) do not allow one to suppose a different Vorlage. Trebolle insists that the references to the blind and lame in vv. 6 and 8 did not belong to the text of Kings used by the Chronicler but are a later gloss[23]. Therefore, it could indeed be an explanatory gloss to clarify the origin of a strange proverb. But in this case the sentence could also have fallen out because of homoioteleuton, either at the stage of the Hebrew transmission (לאמר...לאמר) or at that of the Greek (ὅτι...ὅτι). On the other hand the addition is skillfuly constructed and includes another proverb "ut parva sublimia tangant" that looks like a further literary elaboration. All in all, I am inclined to consider the Old Latin addition to be of a secondary character.

31.—1 Kings 20,15: *Exivit in pugnam et, dispositis his in primis, iussit sequi virtutem reliquam, et videntes speculatores regis Syriae indicaverunt ei.*

There is no trace of this long insertion, which is found in the new material among the marginal glosses recovered for this chapter, neither in the Greek, nor in the Hebrew, the Vulgate, nor in the

---

[20] On the contrary, the marginal notes are very literal in this passage: *Non intrabis huc, quoniam ante te steterunt caeci et claudi dicentes: Non intrabit huc Davit.*
[21] Cf. note 19.
[22] Cf. McCarter, *II Samuel*, p. 135-140.
[23] Cf. J. Trebolle, *Centena in libros Samuelis et Regum*, Madrid 1989, p. 97.

Targum[24]. The content has some affinity with that of v. 17 and v. 19, but fits much better in this sequence of the narrative and there are no signs of midrashic interpretation or of clarifying gloss. Consequently it could belong to the original narrative, but we have no proof to sustain this hypothesis.

32.—2 Kings 20,11: *Ecce ego averto umbram graduum ascensionis, quae descendit in gradus et detenta est in sole.*

Ant: καὶ ἐπέστρεψεν ἡ σκιὰ ἐν τοῖς ἀναβαθμοῖς ᾿Αχὰζ οἷς κατέβη τοὺς δέκα ἀναβαθμοὺς εἰς τὰ ὀπίσω.

MT: הנני משיב את צל המעלות אשר ירדה במעלות אחז בשמש
(Is 38,8)

MT: וישב את הצל במעלות אשר ירדה במעלות אחז אחרנית עשר
(2 Kings 20,11)   מעלות

V: Et reduxit umbram per lineas quibus iam descenderat in horologio Ahaz retrorsum decem gradibus.

He moved the shadow back the ten steps which (the sun) had gone down on the Ahaz dial.

This is a privileged case because we have at our disposal the parallel text of Is 38,8. Using the different texts of both passages for the comparison Catastini has been able to sketch the history of the text in a sequence that stratifies the different witnesses chronologically according to the following pattern: 1Q—LXX Is—MT Is—VL 2 Kings—LXXB 2 Kings—MT 2 Kings[25]. Catastini has shown that the text of the VL reflects a textual stage very close to that of the MT of Isaiah. *Et detenta est in sole* corresponds to the end of the verse אחז בשמש interpreting אחז as a verbal root and not as a proper name. On the other hand *ascensionis* is an ancient reading that goes back to עלית a variant of 1QIs[a].

When—as in this case—a passage is attested by several witnesses we can glimpse the complex process of the text history. Frequently

---

24 The Masoretic Text reads in this verse, "Then Ahab called up these young men, two hundred and thirty-two all told, and behind them the people of Israel, seven thousand in all''.

25 A. Catastini, *Isaia ed Ezechia. Studio di storia della tradizione di II Re 18-20// Is. 36-39*, Roma 1989, p. 269; and —— "Osservazioni filologiche sulla cosidetta 'meridiana di Achaz' (Isaia 38:8// II Re 20: 11)''. *Henoch* 5 (1983) 161-178. See also J. Trebolle, "Old Latin, Old Greek and Old Hebrew in the Books of Kings (1 Ki. 10:27 and 2 Ki. 20:11)''. *Textus* 13 (1986) 85-96.

the text has undergone a complex and multiform transmission, but most of the links in the chain are missing. Consequently, one is tempted to asume that analogically a similar proccess has ocurred elsewhere too. But the text critic has to bee faithful to the evidence, being ready to aknowledge all the changes postulated by the new data, but at the same time refusing to postulate too easily a different *Vorlage* for the singular readings of the Old Latin, when other explanations are also plausible. From this point of view this last example seems to be the exception that confirms the rule.

Conclusions

When I started working on the Old Latin evidence as a witness of the Antiochene text, I was surprised by the number of verses in which the VL was in desagreement with both the Antiochene and the LXX rell. I soon realised that many of those variant readings— sometimes a whole verse or half a verse—were missing in the Hebrew and likewise in the Vulgate too. I thought that the presence of these 'different' texts did not lack interest in the framework of the textual plurality well attested for Samuel-Kings through the Qumran documents. Moreover we were dealing with a *corpus* of well attested texts, not with tiny fragmentary evidence, reconstructed data or unpublished material. Consequently, I thought it would be worthwhile to go further into research on those texts.

I have tried to analyse in detail the most important part of these divergent texts in the light of the evidence known to us in Hebrew, Greek, Latin and the Aramaic Targumim of Samuel-Kings, including the consultation of the Medieval Hebrew manuscripts for those books. I have realised that:

a) A good number of these singular readings are not really such, but could be explained either as double readings or as double sentences constructed out of double readings, or as readings generated by corruptions in the text transmission. These results do not militate against the literalism of the Old Latin translation but are evidence in favour of a literalism that is willing, for the sake of clarity or of a more precise translation, to incorporate into the narrative alternative readings coming from different sources[26]. Very often these

---

[26] "The alternative reading—says Weingreen—must have been written in as a

aberrant texts could be explained as proceeding from the Greek and Latin textual tradition known to us. But sometimes the Greek and Latin links were missing and we had to have recourse to the Hebrew *Vorlage* to explain the genesis of such readings. This circumstance has led us to an important conclusion: that the translators had access to a much richer textual tradition than we have with our surviving manuscripts[27].

b) A second proportion of the divergent texts bear witness to a considerable literary creativity by the translators that led them to use the linguistic resources of the Latin, especially its stylistic devices (*parallelismus membrorum*, chiasm, poliptoton, alliteration, rhythm and sonority) to improve the translation. To my mind, this stylistic interest is not opposed to the literalism of the translation but serves the same aim, to produce a precise and intelligible translation. Rather than attribute the effects of these apparently contradictory translation techniques to diverse components of the material incorporated to the glosses[28], what they really mean is, in my opinion, that the translators were not as illiterate as has been thought in the past.

---

textual note above the accepted reading and was some time later incorporated into the text by a copyist", cf. Weingreen, *Introduction*, p. 86. One can find the confirmation of such a procedure in 5QDt, cf. N. Fernández Marcos, "5QDt y los tipos textuales bíblicos". In *Estudios en honor de José María Casciaro*, Universidad de Navarra, Pamplona 1994, 119-125. This kind of expansion can be best understood whithin a specially developed pattern such as occurs with the Septuagint of Proverbs: "It is obvious that divergences of this type between MT and LXX Prov. do not come from a Hebrew original used by the translator and deviating from MT. They are, instead, stylistical devices deliberately used by the translator. In a Hebrew text the dislike of synonymous parallels, as well as the predilection for sharp antitheses, parisosis etc. remains unintelligible, whereas they are easily understood when connected with the translator's familiarity with Greek literary tradition. It is in accordance with this literary tradition that the translator has, sometimes rather roughly, remoulded his original", cf. G. Gerleman, *Studies in the Septuagint III. Proverbs*, Lund 1956, p. 25-26. Cf. also K.G. O'Connell, "Texts and Versions" in *The New Jerome Biblical Commentary*, New Jersey 1990, p. 1093.

[27] They finished their work before the Bibles destruction under Diocletian (285-305), the Christian recensions of the IVth century A.D. and the diffusion of the ecclesiastical texts under Constantine. Cf. F.C. Burkitt, *The Old Latin and the Itala*. Texts and Studies IV/3, Cambridge 1896, p. 5: "...the value of a version which in its origin at least was utterly independent of the eclectic Greek texts of the fourth century becomes more evident than ever".

[28] As suggested, for instance, by H. Quentin, *Mémoire sur l'établissement du texte de la Vulgate. Ière Partie Octateuque*, Roma-Paris 1922, p. 333: "De ces constatations il ressort que les notes marginales du *Legionensis* sont tirées de plusieurs documents différents. Quels étaient-ils? Ce sera la tâche des futurs éditeurs de les désigner plus exactement si cela est possible".

They were bilingual writers coming from cultivated circles in North Africa or Syria[29].

c) A third class of variant readings consists of very ancient material that betrays traces of having been in contact with a Hebrew tradition, other than the Hexaplaric. It is another question if those contacts were made directly or, as is more plausible, through a Greek *Vorlage* now lost. But it has to be stressed that there are very few cases where we are bound to accept that the different readings of the Old Latin point to a different Hebrew *Vorlage*.

These results may have some consequences in appraising the value of the Old Latin of Kings and its use for text critical purposes. As we have seen the percentage of Old Latin divergent readings has been greatly reduced by means of textual criticism. But textual criticism still has to play a very important role in the purification of material that has suffered a long and complicated transmission through the stages of three different languages[30]. On the one hand

---

[29] Cf. for instance H. Rönsch, *Itala und Vulgata. Das Sprachidiom der urchristlichen Itala und der katholichen Vulgata unter Berücksichtigung der römischen Volkssprache*, Marburg 1875[2], p. 5, P. Capelle, *Le texte du Psautier latin en Afrique*, Rome 1913, p. 183: "Bref, c'est une langue assez rude; elle accuse son origine peu littéraire et vient témoigner à sa manière que la version latine primitive ne fut qu'une éclosion spontanée de la vie et de la piété des peuples chrétiens", G. Bardy, *La question des langues dans l'église ancienne*, Paris 1948, p. 60: "La version africaine de la Bible trahit d'ailleurs son origine populaire"; or more recently McKenzie in *Dictionary of the Bible*, New York 1975[10], 917: "No great merit can be attributed to the Old Latin. It was made from the LXX and the translators had little Latin and less Greek. It was slavishly literal and often unintelligible. The translators were not educated men and produced without intending it one of the greatest monuments of vulgar un-lettered Latin of the period" (cf. B. Kedar, "The Latin Translations" p. 307). But for the cultural niveau of the translators claim U. Rapallo, *Calchi Ebraici nelle Antiche Versioni del "Levitico"*, Rome 1971, p. 19; S. Boscherini, "Sulla lingua delle primitive versioni latine dell' Antico Testamento". *Atti e memorie dell'Accademia Toscana di scienze e Lettere. La Colombaria* 26 (1961-62) 207-229; A. Ceresa-Gastaldo, *Il latino delle antique versioni bibliche*, Roma 1975; E. Valgiglio, *Le antiche versioni latine del Nuovo Testamento. Fedeltà e aspetti grammaticali*, Napoli 1985, and especially Ch. Mohrmann, "Linguistic Problems in the Early Christian Church". *VC* 11 (1957) 11-36, p. 28. Concerning the Old Latin translation of Luke 1,28 χαῖρε κεχαριτωμένη by "gratificata" face to the "gratia plena" of the Vulgate, she comments: "This example, which could be multiplied by many others, may serve to show, that the old process, when intelligently applied, really led to good results, and that one cannot dismiss the early Bible translations as clumsy products of semi-illiterates, as is too often done in classically minded philological circles".

[30] "Lat is the repository of a great many elements of very diverse origin; some of these are valuable, some are not, but it is *only* possible to judge which are valuable

it has been shown to be a very literal version capable of reproducing even the mistakes of the Antiochene (e.g. ἀρχιέταιρος translated in the Old Latin by *princeps amicorum David* instead of 'Hushai the Archite' in the Masoretic Text; 'Archi, David's friend' in LXX rel cf. 2 Sam 15,32). But on the other hand this literalism cannot be pressed too hard because the translators also demonstrate high literary skill with a sophistication far removed from that of a popular version. Their translation constitutes the first attempt to create a Biblical (and Christian) Latin, as can bee seen not only in the numerous neologisms but also in the enormous creativity shown in the style and composition itself. The effort, as stressed by Mohrmann, was gigantic because Christian Latin had, linguistically speaking, to begin from nothing.

Perhaps this phenomenon is not as singular as it would appear at first sight within Biblical text transmission. Is it so different from some translation of the Septuagint in books like Job (abreviations), Proverbs (adaptations), Daniel or Esther (substantial additions)?[31]. In other words, we should not project anachronistically to the IInd century A.D. an image of the Biblical text that in fact proceeds from the diffusion of the ecclesiastical Bibles two centuries later. No doubt we would like to know more about the origin and circumstances, sociological as well as religious, that brought forth the Old Latin, but the lack of evidence in the ancient sources is absolute if we except a few pejorative remarks of Jerome and Augustine always within the context of the new version, the latin Vulgate[32].

---

on purely internal grounds", cf. S. Brock, *The Recensions*, p. 222. According to Satterthwaite, some additions found in the Old Latin and the Greek manuscripts *KZglnow* of Brooke-McLean in the book of Judges are of secondary character too, "that is, they tell us more about the history of exegesis of Ju 20-21 than they do about the original Hebrew text of this passage", cf. P.E. Satterthwaite, "Some Septuagintal Pluses in Judges 20 and 21". *IOSCS* 24 (1991) 25-35, p. 35.

[31] As Gribomont says: "Pour apprécier les libertés de ce genre, il faut considérer, que l'extraordinaire fidélité, que nous pouvons contrôler chez les copistes hébreux à partir de l'ère chrétienne, ne peut être présumée à une époque antérieure, losque la communauté expérimentait encore une phase créative, stimulée par les crises contemporaines et l'attente eschatologique", cf. J. Gribomont, "Aux origines de la Vulgate". In *La Bibbia "Vulgata" dalle origini ai nostri giorni*, Vatican 1987, 11-20, p. 12. And on p. 16: "Tant que la connaissance du grec fut largement répandue, chacun amenda à son aise, comme si le latin n'avait autorité qu'en raison du grec sous-jacent".

[32] For instance we find no traces of the Old Latin being used in the Judaeo-Christian polemic as the Septuagint was. On the riot of Oea (modern Tripoli) against Jerome's new Latin version, cf. Augustine, *epist.* LXXI, in Migne, *PL* XXXIII, p. 241-243.

As for the problem sketched earlier of the contribution of the Old Latin to the present discussion on textual pluralism in the books of Kings, it is important to bear in mind in conclusion: a) that the number of divergent readings has been greatly reduced and b) that only in a few cases can they be shown to be connected with a different Hebrew text.

However in spite of these cautions it must be recognised that several Old Latin readings bear witness to a Hebrew text different from the Masoretic one, firstly because the Old Latin follows the Antiochene text as its main *Vorlage*, a text in many aspects diverse from the Masoretic for Samuel-Kings, and, secondly, because the Old Latin attests some variants of the Hebrew lost in the rest of the tradition. Therefore, contacts of the Old Latin with the Hebrew tradition are out of doubt. The problem arises with the interpretation of those contacts. Authors like Blondheim, Baumstark, Sparks, Cassuto, Schildenberger have claimed for a Hebrew original as the ultimate source of the Old Latin[33]. But we have no evidence of pre-Christian Latin translations made from the Hebrew, and even the Septuagint at that time began to fall into disuse among the Jews[34]. The need of the Latin in the liturgy of the synagogues of North Africa is to be expected as a consequence of the linguistic change from Greek to Latin. But precisely the language spoken among the North Africa Jews was at that time the Greek and not the Hebrew as witness the

---

[33] D.S. Blondheim, *Les parlers Judéo-romans et la* Vetus Latina, Paris 1925, p. XXXIV-LXIX; A. Baumstark, "Neue orientalische Probleme biblischer Textgeschichte". *ZDMG* 89 (1935) 89-118; H.F.D. Sparks, "The Latin Bible", in H.W. Robinson (ed.) *The Bible in its Ancient and English Versions*, London 1954[2], p. 100-127; U. Cassuto, "The Jewish Translations of the Bible into Latin and its importance for the Study of the Greek and Aramaic Versions" in *Biblical and Oriental Studies 1*, Jerusalem 1973, p. 285-299 and J. Schildenberger, *Die altlateinische Texte des Proverbien-Buches I*, Beuron 1941, p. 139-143. For a slight different approach to the same subject cf. J. Cantera, "La Vetus Latina y el texto masorético. Hipótesis de una revisión de la Vetus Latina a base del texto hebreo". *Sefarad* 23 (1963) 252-264, and ――, "Puntos de contacto de la Vetus Latina con el Targum arameo y con la Peshitta. Hipótesis de un origen targúmico de la Vetus Latina". *Sefarad* 25 (1965) 1-18.

[34] Cf. B. Kedar, "The Latin Translations", p. 309 and J. Gribomont, "Les plus anciennes traductions latines de la Bible", in *Le monde latin antique et la Bible*, ed. by J. Fontaine and Ch. Pietri, Paris 1985, 43-65, p. 46: "Rien ne suggère qu'on doive remonter aux communautés juives, qui étaient particulièrement orientalisées".

documents contained in the *Corpus Papyrorum Judaicarum* and the *Corpus Inscriptionum Judaicarum.*[35]

On the other hand, we have realised that the contacts of the Old Latin with the Hebrew, particularly the Hebrew transliterations, are not systematic but focus on special chapters and passages. Otherwise it would be impossible to explain the frequency of cases in which the Old Latin has tried to produce a new meaning in a difficult passage quite far from the Masoretic Text and that of the Vulgate. Many of the Old Latin singular readings, sometimes whole sentences, are inner Latin developments going from the Greek tradition but without connection with the Hebrew and, as a matter of fact, with the Vulgate[36].

In brief, these considerations preclude any use of the Old Latin for the restoration of the Biblical text and for the discussion of textual pluralism until it has been first critically examined according to the proper criteria of inner textual criticism.

In all probability only when this task has been accomplished will it be meaningful to ask further questions, concerning such matters as the unity or plurality of the translation, its Jewish or Christian origin, the explanation of its intermittent Hebraisms etc.[37]

---

[35] *Corpus Papyrorum Judaicarum*, I and II ed. by V.A. Tcherikover and A. Fuks, Cambridge Mass. 1957 and 1960; III ed. by V.A. Tcherikover, A. Fuks and M. Stern, Cambridge Mass. 1964. *Corpus Inscriptionum Judaicarum*, ed. by J.B. Frey, I *Europe*, Roma 1936; II *Asie-Afrique*, Roma 1952. According to the epigraphical documents the Greek prevails in Rome until the beginning of the 4th Century A.D., while in North Africa the Christian Latin literature appears since the end of the 2nd Century A.D., cf. J. Gribomont, "Les plus anciennes traductions latines de la Bible", p. 46.

[36] I am inclined to think that the Old Latin is certainly rooted in the Hebrew. But in all probability, some of the so-called Old Latin "Hebraisms" came to the translators through their Greek *Vorlage* while others were the result of continuous revisions of the Old Latin according to the different texts of the Septuagint that were circulating in the different regions, in the same way that the Septuagint was revised in accordance with the Hebrew text available. In addition, the influence of the three younger translators (Aquila-Symmachus-Theodotion) on the Old Latin is apparent, be it *via* Hexapla, or prior to the composition of the Hexapla. The Old Latin translators had access to many more Greek texts than those we know through the extant manuscripts, those being texts that could contain the inherited "Hebraisms".

[37] Perhaps the dilemma Jewish or Christian is not so important inasmuch as Jews and Christians used the Septuagint alike until the 2nd century A.D. and probably the substitution by other Greek translations did not succeed in all the geographical areas at the same time. Besides, as pointed out by Daniélou, there is the problem of the Judaeo-Christians whose chronological limits are not easy to outline, cf. J. Daniélou, *Les origines du Christianisme latin*, Paris 1978, p. 116-117.

BIBLIOGRAPHY

Allen, L.C., "Further thoughts on an old recension of Reigns in Paralipomena". *HTR* 61 (1968) 483-491.

——, *The Greek Chronicles I-II. VTS 25-26*, Leiden 1974.

Aptowitzer, V., "Rabbinische Parallelen und Aufschlüsse zu LXX und Vg: I, Die Bücher Samuelis". *ZAW* 29 (1909) 241-252.

Ayuso, T., "Los elementos extrabíblicos de los libros de los Reyes". *EstBib* 4 (1945) 259-296.

——, *La Vetus Latina Hispana I. Prolegómenos*, Madrid 1953.

——, *La Vetus Latina Hispana 2. El Octateuco*, Madrid 1967.

Bardy, G., *Recherches sur St. Lucien et son école*, Paris 1936.

——, *La question des langues dans l'église ancienne*, Paris 1948.

Barthélemy, D., "Redécouverte d'un chaînon manquant de l'histoire de la LXX". *RB* 60 (1953) 18-29.

——, *Les Devanciers d'Aquila. VTS* 10 (1963).

——, *Critique textuelle de l'Ancien Testament. 1 Josué, Juges, Ruth, Samuel, Rois, Chroniques, Esdras, Néhémie, Esther*, Fribourg/Göttingen 1982.

Barthélemy, D., Gooding, D.W., Lust, J., Tov, E., *The Story of David and Goliath. Textual and Literary Criticism*, Fribourg/Göttingen 1986.

Blondheim, D.S., *Les parlers judéo-romans et la Vetus Latina. Études sur les rapports entre les traductions bibliques en langue romane des Juifs au moyen âge et les anciennes versions*, Paris 1925.

Boer, P.A.H., *Research into the Text of I Samuel (I-XVI)*, Amsterdam 1938.

——, "I Samuel XVII. Notes on the text and the ancient versions". *OTS* I (1941/2) 79-103.

——, "Research into the text of I Samuel XVIII-XXXI". *OTS* 6 (1949) 1-100.

Brock, S.P., *The Recensions of the Septuagint Version ef 1 Samuel*, Diss. Oxford 1966.

——, "Lucian *redivivus*: Some Reflections on Barthélemy's *Les Devanciers d'Aquila*". *Studia Evangelica V = TU* 103, Berlin 1968, 305-310.

——, "Origen's aims as a Textual Critic of the Old Testament". *Studia Patristica X*, ed. F.L. Cross = *TU* 107, Berlin 1970, 215-218.

——, "A Doublet and its Ramifications". *Bib* 56 (1975) 550-556.

——, "Aspects of Translation Technique in Antiquity". *Greek, Roman and Byzantine Studies* 20 (1979) 69-87.

Busto Saiz, J.R., "On the Lucianic Manuscripts in 1-2 Kings". *VI Congress of the IOSCS*, edited by C. Cox, Atlanta, Georgia 1987, 305-310.

Cantera, J., "Puntos de contacto de la 'Vetus Latina' con la recension de Luciano y con otras recensiones griegas". *Sefarad* 25 (1965) 69-72.

Catastini, A., *Isaia ed Ezechia. Studio di storia della tradizione di II Re 18-20//Is 36-39*, Roma 1989.

Chiesa, B., "Appunti di storia della critica del testo dell'Antico Testamento ebraico". *Henoch* 12 (1990) 3-15.

Cogan, M.-Tadmor, H., *II Kings. A New Translation with Introduction and Commentary*, The Anchor Bible 11, New York 1988.

Cross, F.M., "The History of the Biblical Text in the Light of Discoveries in the Judaean Desert". *HTR* 57 (1964) 281-299.

Cross, F.M.-Talmon, S., *Qumran and the History of the Biblical Text*, Cambridge Mass. 1975.

Daniélou, J., *Les origines du Christianisme latin*, Paris 1978.

Deboys, D.G., *The Greek Text of 2 Kings*, Diss. Oxford 1981.

——, "Recensional Criteria in the Greek Text of II Kings". *JSS* 31 (1986) 135-139.

De Bruyne, D., "Études sur les origines de la Vulgate en Espagne". *RevBén* 31 (1914-19) 373-401.

Devreesse, R. *Les anciens commentateurs grecs de l'Octateuque et des Rois (Fragments tirés des chaînes). ST 201*, Vatican 1959.

——, *Le commentaire de Théodore de Mopsueste sur les Psaumes. ST 93*, Vatican 1939.

Dieu, L., "Retouches lucianiques sur quelques textes de la Vieille Latine (I et II Samuel)". *RB ns* 16 (1919) 372-403.

——, "Les manuscrits grecs des livres de Samuel". *Le Muséon* 34 (1921) 17-60.

Dörrie, H., "Zur Geschichte der LXX im Jahrhundert Konstantins". *ZNW* 39 (1940) 57-110.

Driver, S.R., *Notes on the Hebrew Text and Topography of the Books of Samuel*, Oxford 1913².

Fernández Marcos, N., "El protoluciánico ¿revisión griega de los judíos de Antioquía?". *Bib* 64 (1983) 423-427.

——, "The Lucianic Text in the Books of Kingdoms: From Lagarde to the Textual Pluralism". *De Septuaginta. Studies in Honour of John William Wevers on his sixty-fifth birthday*, edited by A. Pietersma and C. Cox, Toronto/Brandon 1984, 161-175.

——, "On the Present State of Septuagint Research in Spain". *La Septuaginta en la investigación contemporánea (V Congreso de la IOSCS)*, edited by N. Fernández Marcos, Madrid 1985, 271-285.

——, "Literary and Editorial Features of the Antiochian Text in Kings. *VI Congress of the IOSCS*, edited by C. Cox, Atlanta, Georgia 1987, 287-304.

——, "Some Reflections on the Antiochian Text of the Septuagint". *Studien zur Septuaginta—Robert Hanhart zu Ehren*, edited by D. Fraenkel, U. Quast and John W. Wevers, Göttingen 1990, 219-230.

——, "The Antiochian Text in I-II Chronicles". *VII Congres of the IOSCS*, edited by C. Cox, Atlanta, Georgia 1992, 301-311.

Fernández Marcos, N.-Busto Saiz, J.R., *El texto antioqueno de la Biblia griega. I, 1-2 Samuel*, Madrid 1989; *II, 1-2 Reyes*, Madrid 1992.

Fischer, B., "Lukian-Lesarten in der Vetus Latina der Vier Königsbücher". *Studia Anselmiana* 27/8 (1951) 169-177.

Gooding, D.W., *Relics of Ancient Exegesis. A Study of the Miscellanies in 3 Reigns 2.*, Cambridge 1976.

——, "An Appeal for a Stricter Terminology in the Textual Criticism of the Old Testament". *JSS* 21 (1976) 15-25.

Goshen-Gottstein, M.H., "Theory and Practice of Textual Criticism. The Text-critical Use of the Septuagint". *Textus* 3 (1963) 130-158.

——, "The Book of Samuel—Hebrew and Greek—Hindsight of a Century". *Textus* XIV (1988) 147-161.

Gribomont, J., "Les plus anciennes traductions latines de la Bible". *Le monde latin antique et la Bible*, edited by J. Fontaine and Ch. Pietri, Paris 1985, 43-65.

Hanhart, R., "Zum gegenwärtigen Stand der Septuagintaforschung". *De Septuaginta. Studies in honour of John William Wevers*, 3-18.

Johnson, B., *Die hexaplarische Rezension des 1. Samuelbuches der Septuaginta*, Lund 1963.

——, *Die armenische Bibelübersetzung als hexaplarischer Zeuge im 1. Samuelbuch*, Lund 1968.

Kahle, P., "Der gegenwärtige Stand der Erforschung der in Palästina neu gefundenen hebräischen Handschriften". *TLZ* 79 (1954) 81-94.

——, *The Cairo Geniza*, Oxford 1959[2].

——, "The Greek Bible and the Fragments from the Judaean Desert". *Studia Evan-gelica 1 = TU 73*, Berlin 1959, 613-621.

Kedar, B., "The Latin Translations". *Mikra. Text, Translations, Reading and Inter-pretation of the Hebrew Bible in Ancient Judaism and Early Christianity*, edited by M.J. Mulder, Van Gorcum 1988, 299-338.

Klein, R.W., *Textual Criticism of the Old Testament*, Philadelphia 1974.

Kyle McCarter, P., *I Samuel. A New Translation with Introduction and Commentary*. The Anchor Bible 8, New York 1984[4].

——, *II Samuel. A New Translation with Introduction and Commentary*. The Anchor Bible 9, New York 1984[3].

Lagarde, P., *Librorum Veteris Testamenti Canonicorum Pars Prior Graece*, Göttingen 1883.

Mercati, G., "Di alcune testimonianze antiche sulle cure bibliche di San Luciano". *Bib* 24 (1943) 1-17.

Metzger, B.M., "The Lucianic Recension of the Greek Bible". *Chapters in the His-tory of New Testament textual Criticism*, Leiden 1963, 1-41.

Mohrmann, Ch., "Linguistic Problems in the Early Christian Church". *VC* 11 (1957) 11-36.

Montgomery, J.A.-Gehman, H.S., *A Critical and Exegetical Commentary on the Books of Kings*, Edinburgh 1951.

Moore, G.F., "The Antiochian recension of the LXX". *AJSL* 29 (1912/13) 37-62.

Morano Rodríguez, C., *Glosas marginales de Vetus Latina en Biblias Vulgatas españolas. 1-2 Samuel*, Madrid 1989.

Moreno Hernández, A., *Las glosas marginales de Vetus Latina en las Biblias Vulgatas españolas. 1-2 Reyes*, Madrid 1992.

Muraoka, T., "The Greek Texts of Samuel-Kings: Incomplete Translation or Recensional Activity?". *Abr-Naharain* 21 (1982-83) 28-49.

Pietersma, A., "Proto-Lucian and the Greek Psalter". *VT* 28 (1978) 66-72.

Pisano, S., *Additions or Omissions in the Books of Samuel*, Fribourg/Göttingen 1984.

Rahlfs, A., *Septuaginta-Studien 1. Studien zu den Königsbüchern*, Göttingen 1904.

——, *Septuaginta-Studien 3. Lucians Rezension der Königsbüchern*, Göttingen 1911.

——, *Paul de Lagardes wissenschaftliches Lebenswerk im Rahmen einer Geschichte seines Lebens dargestellt*, Göttingen 1928.

Rehm, M., *Textkritische Untersuchungen zu den Parallelstellen der Samuel-Königsbücher und der Chronik. ATA* XII, 3 (1937).

Seeligmann, L., "Indications of editorial alteration and adaptation in the MT and in the Septuagint". *VT* 11 (1961) 201-221.

Shenkel, J.D., *Chronology and Recensional Development in the Greek Text of Kings*, Cam-bridge Mass. 1968.

Skehan, P.W., "The Biblical Scrolls from Qumran and the Text of the Old Testa-ment". *BA* 28 (1965) 87-100.

Spanneut, M., "La Bible d'Eustathe d'Antioche—contribution à l'histoire de la 'version lucianique'". *Studia Patristica 4 = TU 79*, Berlin 1961, 171-190.

Spottorno Díaz-Caro, M.-V., "Some Remarks on Josephus' Biblical Text". *VI Congress of the IOSCS*, 277-285.

——, "Flavio Josefo. Técnicas de adaptación del texto bíblico". *Sefarad* 52 (1992) 227-234.

Stoebe, H.J., "Die Goliathperikope I Sam. XVII:1—XVIII:5 und die Textform der LXX". *VT* 6 (1956) 397-413.

Talmon, S., "Synonymous Readings in the Textual Tradition of the Old Testa-ment". *ScrHier* 8 (1961) 335-385.

——, "Between the Bible and the Mishnah: Qumran from Within". *Jewish Civili-*

zation in the Hellenistic-Roman Period, ed. by S. Talmon, Sheffield 1991, 214-257.

Talshir, Z., "Double Translations in the Septuagint". *VI Congress of the IOSCS*, 21-63.

——, "The Representation of the Divine Epithet *Zeba'ot* in the Septuagint and the Accepted Division of the Books of Kingdoms". *JQR* 78 (1987) 57-75.

Thackeray, H.St.J., "The Greek Translators of the Four Books of Kings". *JThS* 8 (1907) 262-278.

——, *The Septuagint and Jewish Worship*, London 1923².

——, *Josephus. The Man and the Historian*, New York 1929.

Thornhill, R., "Six or seven Nations: A pointer to the Lucianic Text in the Heptateuch with special reference to the Old Latin Version". *JThS, ns.* 10 (1959) 233-246.

Tisserant, E., *Codex Zuqninensis Rescriptus Veteris Testamenti. ST 23*, Roma 1911.

Tov, E. (ed.), *The Hebrew and Greek Texts of Samuel*, Jerusalem 1980.

——, "Lucian and proto-Lucian. Toward a New Solution of the Problem". *RB* 79 (1972) 101-113.

——, "The Textual Affiliations of 4QSamᵃ". *JSOT* 14 (1979) 37-53.

Trebolle Barrera, J., *Salomón y Jeroboam. Historia de la recensión y redacción de 1 Reyes 2-12,14*, Salamanca-Jerusalem 1980.

——, *Jehú y Joás. Texto y composición literaria de 2 Reyes 9-11*, Valencia 1980.

——, *Centena in libros Samuelis et Regum*, Madrid 1989.

Ulrich, E., *The Qumran Text of Samuel and Josephus*, Missoula, Montana 1978.

——, "Horizons of Old Testament Textual Research at the Thirtieth Anniversary of Qumran Cave 4". *CBQ* 46 (1984) 613-636.

Van der Woude, A.S., "Pluriformity and Uniformity. Reflections on the Transmission of the Text of the Old Testament". *Sacred History and Sacred Texts in Early Judaism*. A Symposium in Honour of A.S. van der Woude, J.N. Bremmer and F. García Martínez (editors), Kampen 1992, 151-169.

Vercellone, C., *Variae lectiones Vulgatae Latinae bibliorum editionis*, I, Roma 1860; II, Roma 1864.

Weingreen, J., *Introduction to the Critical Study of the Text of the Hebrew Bible*, Oxford 1982.

Wellhausen, J., *Der Text der Bücher Samuelis*, Göttingen 1871.

Wendland, P., "Zur ältesten Geschichte der Bibel in der Kirche". *ZAW* 1 (1900) 267-290.

West, M.L., *Textual Criticism and Editorial Technique applicable to Greek and Latin texts*, Stuttgart 1973.

Wevers, J.W., "A Study in the Hebrew Variants in the Books of Kings". *ZAW* 61 (1945-48) 42-76.

——, "A Study in the exegetical principles of the translator of II Sam. XI: 2—I Kings II: 11". *CBQ* 15 (1953) 30-45.

——, "Theodoret's *Quaest* and the Byzantine Text". *Henoch* 13 (1991) 29-64.

INDEXES

I. Index of Authors

II. Index of Biblical References

III. Index of Other Sources

IV. Index of Greek Words

V. Index of Hebrew Words

VI. Index of Latin words

PLATES

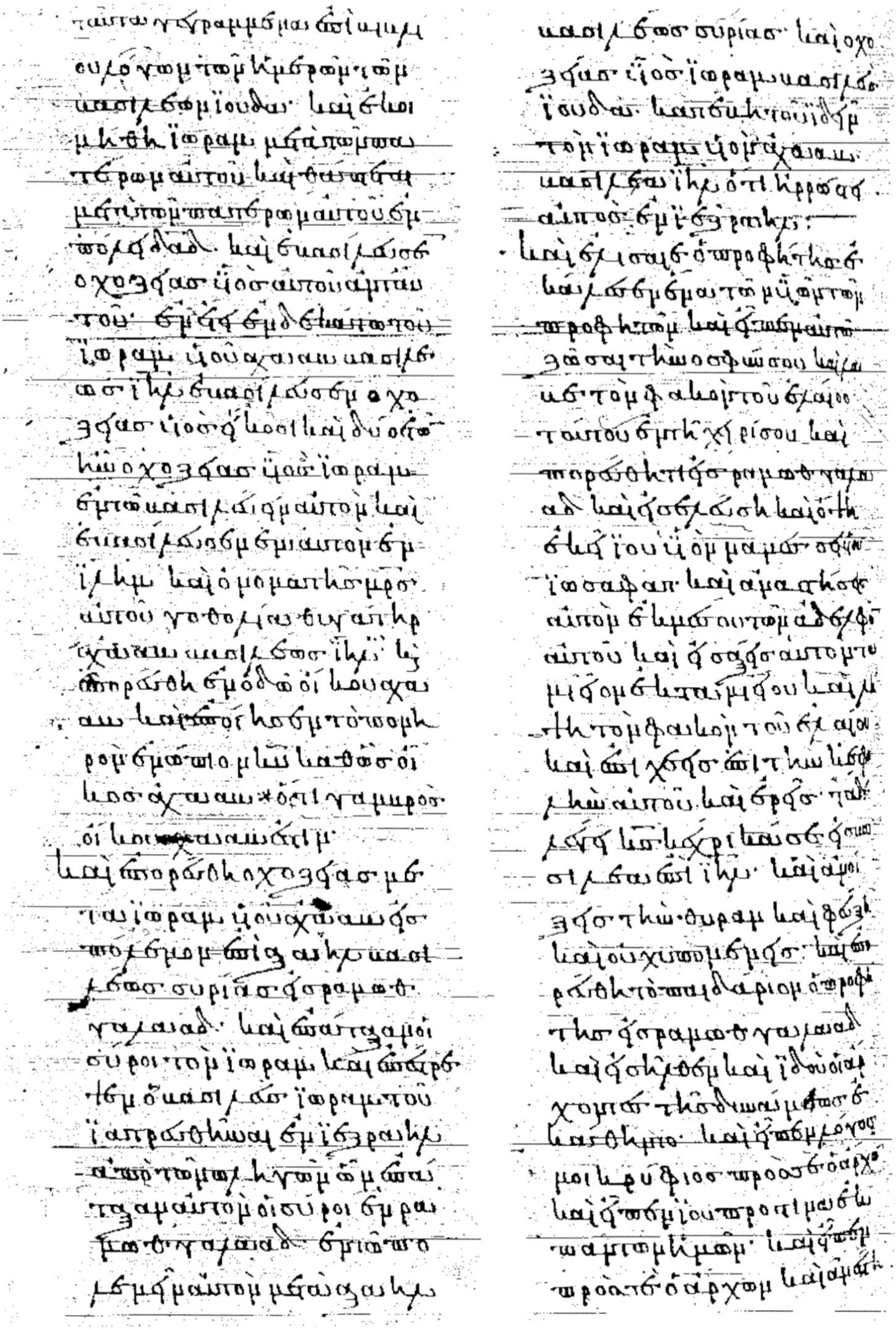

Figure 1. Moscow, Synodal Library (today Historical Museum) Gr. 31, early X century, ff. 361ᵛ–362ʳ.

Figure 2. (a) f. 119ʳ; Léon (Spain), *Codex Gothicus Legionensis*, A.D. 960: A Vulgate Bible with Old Latin Marginal Glosses and Miniatures.

Figure 2. (b) f. 121ʳ; Léon (Spain), *Codex Gothicus Legionensis*, A.D. 960: A Vulgate Bible with Old Latin Marginal Glosses and Miniatures.

Figure 2. (c) f. 127ᵛ; Léon (Spain), *Codex Gothicus Legionensis,* A.D. 960: A Vulgate Bible with Old Latin Marginal Glosses and Miniatures.

Figure 2. (d) f. 146ᵛ; Léon (Spain), *Codex Gothicus Legionensis*, A.D. 960: A Vulgate Bible with Old Latin Marginal Glosses and Miniatures.

Βαβυλῶνος ἐπιστολὰς καὶ δῶρα Ἐζεκία· ἤκουσε γὰρ ὅτι ἠρρώστησεν Ἐζεκίας καὶ ἀνέστη. ¹³ καὶ ἐχάρη ἐπ' αὐτοῖς Ἐζεκίας καὶ ἔδειξεν αὐτοῖς πάντα τὸν οἶκον τῆς ὑπάρξεως αὐτοῦ καὶ τοῦ νεχωθὰ καὶ τὸ ἀργύριον καὶ τὸ χρυσίον καὶ τὰ ἀρώματα καὶ τὸ ἔλαιον τὸ ἀγαθὸν καὶ τὸν οἶκον τῶν σκευῶν αὐτοῦ καὶ πάντα ὅσα εὑρέθη ἐν τοῖς θησαυροῖς, καὶ οὐ παρέλιπεν οὐθὲν ὃ οὐκ ἔδειξεν αὐτοῖς Ἐζεκίας ἐν τῷ οἴκῳ αὐτοῦ καὶ ἐν παντὶ θησαυρῷ αὐτοῦ. ¹⁴ καὶ εἰσῆλθεν Ἠσαίας ὁ προφήτης πρὸς Ἐζεκίαν τὸν βασιλέα καὶ εἶπεν αὐτῷ Τί ἐλάλησαν πρὸς σὲ οἱ ἄνδρες οὗτοι, καὶ πόθεν ἥκουσι πρὸς σέ; καὶ εἶπεν Ἐζεκίας Ἐκ γῆς πόρρωθεν ἥκασι πρὸς μέ, ἐκ Βαβυλῶνος. ¹⁵ καὶ εἶπεν Ἠσαίας Τί εἶδον ἐν τῷ οἴκῳ σου; καὶ εἶπεν Ἐζεκίας Πάντα ὅσα ἐν τῷ οἴκῳ μου εἶδον· οὐκ ἦν ἐν τῷ οἴκῳ μου ὃ οὐκ ἔδειξα αὐτοῖς, ἀλλὰ καὶ τὰ ἐν τοῖς θησαυροῖς μου. ¹⁶ καὶ εἶπεν Ἠσαίας πρὸς Ἐζεκίαν Ἄκουσον τὸν λόγον Κυρίου παντοκράτορος. ¹⁷ ἰδοὺ ἡμέραι ἔρχονται, φησὶ Κύριος, καὶ ἀρθήσεται πάντα τὰ ἐν τῷ οἴκῳ σου καὶ ὅσα ἐθησαύρισαν οἱ πατέρες σου ἕως τῆς ἡμέρας ταύτης· εἰς Βαβυλῶνα ἀπενεχθήσεται, καὶ οὐχ ὑπολειφθήσεται ῥῆμα, εἶπε Κύριος. ¹⁸ καὶ ἀπὸ τῶν υἱῶν σου τῶν ἐξεληλυθότων ἐκ σοῦ, ὧν ἐγέννησας, λήψονται καὶ ποιήσουσι σπάδοντας ἐν τῷ οἴκῳ τοῦ βασιλέως Βαβυλῶνος. ¹⁹ καὶ εἶπεν Ἐζεκίας πρὸς Ἠσαίαν Ἀγαθὸς ὁ λόγος ὃν ἐλάλησε Κύριος· γενέσθω εἰρήνη καὶ δικαιοσύνη ἐν ταῖς ἡμέραις μου. ²⁰ καὶ τὰ λοιπὰ τῶν λόγων Ἐζεκίου καὶ πάντα ὅσα ἐποίησε

---

108   δῶρα Ἐζεκία] βαναὰ πρὸς Ἐζεκίαν 82   >καὶ ἀνέστη — Ἐζεκίας (v. 13)
82   **13** οἶκον post ὑπάρξεως 82   >αὐτοῦ καὶ 82   αὐτοῦ 2.°]   >82: >αὐτῶν
19   >τοῖς 82   θησαυροῖς + αὐτοῦ 82   παρέλιπεν — ὃ] παρῆλθον τόπος ὃν
82   παρέλειπεν 19 108 127   >ἐν τῷ οἴκῳ αὐτοῦ 19   **14** καὶ 1.° sub — 127
Ἐζεκίαν post βασιλέα 82   αὐτῷ] πρὸς αὐτὸν 82   >πρὸς σὲ 82   ἥκουσι] ἥκασι
82   πόρωθεν 108   ἥκασι] ἥκουσι 19 108 127   **15** >Ἠσαίας 82   >Ἐζεκίας
82   >εἶδον — οἴκῳ μου 127· sed habet 127ᵐᵍ   >εἶδον 82   μου 2.° + οὐθὲν
93   >τὰ 19 108 127   **16** Ἠσαίας] Ἐζεκίας 19   Ἐζεκίαν] Ἠσαίαν 19   παντοκρά-
τωρος 82   **17** ἀπενεχθήσονται 93   **18** ἐληλυθότων 82   λήμψονται 82: λήψον 93
ἐπάδοντας 19 108   **19** Κύριος] Κυρίου ante ὃν 82   γενέσθω] ἔστω 82   >καὶ
δικαιοσύνη 82   μου] σου 93   **20** >καὶ πάντα — ἐποίησε 82

καὶ ἀνέστη] ויחיה 1QIsᵃ 39, 1   **13** τῆς ὑπάρξεως αὐτοῦ] נכחיד 1QIsᵃ 39, 2   *Et os-tendit illis omnem domum substantiae suae, et aurum et argentum, et omnem volunta-tem, et odoramina et oleum bonum* L₉₁₋₉₅   **16** παντοκράτορος] צבאות 1QIsᵃ 39, 5   **17** ἀπενεχθήσεται] יבואו 1QIsᵃ 39, 6   **18** λήψονται] יקחו 1QIsᵃ 39, 7   *Et de filiis tuis qui nascentur ex te, tollent et facient eunuchos in domo regis* Hi Jov   **19** Ηὔ-χετο μέχρι τῆς αὐτοῦ ζωῆς εἰρήνην ὑπάρξαι Jos X 34   *Bonum verbum quod locutus est Dominus: fiat pax et fides in diebus meis* Am Jac   *Fiat pax in diebus meis* Hi Am 3.

Figure 3. A page of *The Antiochene Text of the Greek Bible.*

SUPPLEMENTS TO VETUS TESTAMENTUM

35. Krašovec, J. *Antithetic structure in Biblical Hebrew poetry*. 1984. ISBN 90 04 07244 6

36. Emerton, J.A. (ed.). *Congress Volume*, Salamanca 1983. 1985. ISBN 90 04 07281 0

37. Lemche, N.P. *Early Israel*. Anthropological and historical studies on the Israelite society before the monarchy. 1985. ISBN 90 04 07853 3

38. Nielsen, K. *Incense in Ancient Israel*. 1986. ISBN 90 04 07702 2

39. Pardee, D. *Ugaritic and Hebrew poetic parallelism*. A trial cut. 1988. ISBN 90 04 08368 5

40. Emerton, J.A. (ed.). *Congress Volume*, Jerusalem 1986. 1988. ISBN 90 04 08499 1

41. Emerton, J.A. (ed.). *Studies in the Pentateuch*. 1990. ISBN 90 04 09195 5

42. McKenzie, S.L. *The trouble with Kings*. The composition of the Book of Kings in the Deuteronomistic History. 1991. ISBN 90 04 09402 4

43. Emerton, J.A. (ed.). *Congress Volume*, Leuven 1989. 1991. ISBN 90 04 09398 2

44. Haak, R.D. *Habakkuk*. 1992. ISBN 90 04 09506 3

45. Beyerlin, W. *Im Licht der Traditionen*. Psalm LXVII und CXV. Ein Entwicklungszusammenhang. 1992. ISBN 90 04 09635 3

46. Meier, S.A. *Speaking of Speaking*. Marking direct discourse in the Hebrew Bible. 1992. ISBN 90 04 09602 7

47. Kessler, R. *Staat und Gesellschaft im vorexilischen Juda*. Vom 8. Jahrhundert bis zum Exil. 1992. ISBN 90 04 09646 9

48. Auffret, P. *Voyez de vos yeux*. Étude structurelle de vingt psaumes, dont le psaume 119. 1993. ISBN 90 04 09707 4

49. García Martínez, F., A. Hilhorst and C.J. Labuschagne (eds.). *The Scriptures and the Scrolls*. Studies in honour of A.S. van der Woude on the occasion of his 65th birthday. 1992. ISBN 90 04 09746 5

50. Lemaire, A. and B. Otzen (eds.). *History and Traditions of Early Israel*. Studies presented to Eduard Nielsen, May 8th, 1993. 1993. ISBN 90 04 09851 8

51. Gordon, R.P. *Studies in the Targum to the Twelve Prophets*. From Nahum to Malachi. 1994. ISBN 90 04 09987 5

52. Hugenberger, G.P. *Marriage as a Covenant*. A Study of Biblical Law and Ethics Governing Marriage Developed from the Perspective of Malachi. 1994. ISBN 90 04 09977 8

53. García Martínez, F., A. Hilhorst, J.T.A.G.M. van Ruiten, A.S. van der Woude. *Studies in Deuteronomy*. In honour of C.J. Labuschagne on the occasion of his 65th birthday. 1994. ISBN 90 04 10052 0

54. Fernández Marcos, N. *Scribes and Translators*. Septuagint and Old Latin in the Books of Kings. 1994. ISBN 90 04 10043 1

55. Smith, M.S. *The Ugaritic Baal Cycle. Volume I*. Introduction with Text, Translation and Commentary of KTU 1.1-1.2. 1994. ISBN 90 04 09995 6

56. Duguid, I.M. *Ezekiel and the Leaders of Israel*. 1994. ISBN 90 04 10074 1